Business Intelligence with Looker Cookbook

Create BI solutions and data applications to explore and share insights in real time

Khrystyna Grynko

Business Intelligence with Looker Cookbook

Copyright © 2024 Packt Publishing

Group Product Manager: Kaustubh Manglurkar
Publishing Product Manager: Heramb Bhavsar
Book Project Manager: Kirti Pisat
Senior Editor: Gowri Rekha
Technical Editor: Seemanjay Ameriya
Copy Editor: Safis Editing
Proofreader: Gowri Rekha
Indexer: Pratik Shirodkar
Production Designer: Prafulla Nikalje
DevRel Marketing Coordinator: Nivedita Singh

First published: May 2024
Production reference: 1190424

Published by Packt Publishing Ltd.

Grosvenor House
11 St Paul's Square
Birmingham
B3 1RB, UK

ISBN 978-1-80056-095-6
www.packtpub.com

To the entire Looker team – both the creators and those who constantly work to make it better

– thank you.

Contributors

About the author

Khrystyna Grynko is a data analyst and Looker expert with over 10 years of experience. She is passionate about helping businesses use data to make better decisions.

Khrystyna began her career as a digital marketer. She quickly realized the power of data to drive business decisions and decided to pursue a career in data analysis.

After graduating from Lumière University Lyon 2 with a Master's degree in BI, Khrystyna worked as a data analyst at several companies, where she helped businesses use data to solve real-world problems.

Khrystyna is a frequent speaker at industry events and has written numerous articles on data and Looker. She is also a mentor and coach to other data professionals. With a passion for teaching, Khrystyna is both an author of an online BigQuery course and a lecturer at multiple French universities and business schools.

About the reviewers

Maire Newton is an outbound product manager for Looker at Google Cloud and an expert in data modeling and visualization. She's passionate about helping customers develop data-driven cultures by using technology to meet users where they are. As a former consultant, Maire has over 15 years of experience partnering with organizations to develop data solutions and drive digital transformation.

Boris Glazman is a pre-sales engineer with an extensive background in the architecture of data and advanced analytics solutions, machine learning, and BI.

The first 15 years of his career he spent on Wall Street and in the City of London developing trading, middle-, and back-office systems for the biggest investment banks and wealth management institutions. When he moved to Paris, he began working with software vendors, primarily on all things data, BI, and machine learning.

Currently, Boris works at Google Cloud as a member of the Expert Data and Analytics Customer Engineering team, specializing in Looker. A major part of his job is to act as a technical advocate for Google Cloud prospects and customers.

Alex Christiansen is a customer engineer at Google, specializing in the Looker platform. With over four years of experience, he thrives on finding technical solutions to empower his customers. When not at work, Alex embraces the outdoors through running, golfing, snowboarding, and traveling.

Luka Fontanilla is a data product and AI solutions professional with a strong passion for helping organizations unlock the full potential of their data assets. He specializes in crafting data-driven application experiences that deliver tangible value. His expertise includes developing robust data monetization strategies and seamlessly integrating AI capabilities to empower client-facing applications.

Skander Larbi is a data analytics and AI solutions leader at Google Cloud, helping global clients transform ideas into market-leading products. With a focus on strategic results since joining Looker in 2017, he drives GTM success, sales growth, and pre-sales initiatives for clients ranging from innovative startups to Fortune-500 companies and international powerhouses.

Table of Contents

2

Configuring Views and Models in a LookML Project   45

3

Working with Data in Explores   81

4

Customizing and Serving Dashboards   109

5

Making Dashboards Interactive through Dynamic Elements   125

6

Troubleshooting Looker   145

7

Integrating Looker with Other Applications   163

10

Preparing to Develop Looker Applications   209

Preface

This book offers a comprehensive guide to mastering Looker, a powerful cloud-based business intelligence platform. You'll learn the fundamentals of setting up your Looker account and creating LookML projects, along with the art of exploring data and crafting impactful dashboards. Additionally, the book delves into advanced techniques including dashboard interactivity, troubleshooting, application development, content organization, and seamless integration with other tools. By the end, you'll have the skills to harness Looker's full potential for data analysis, visualization, and customized data-driven solutions.

Who this book is for

This book is the perfect guide for beginners wanting to master business intelligence with Looker, offering step-by-step instructions for navigating the platform. It will teach you how to master Looker's powerful features to solve business problems and make smarter decisions.

This book offers a beginner-friendly yet thorough introduction to Looker, making it perfect for data analysts, BI engineers, data scientists, and anyone eager to explore data modeling, visualization, analysis, and reporting with Looker.

Due to the newness of Looker's latest AI features and limited availability, they are not included in this book.

What this book covers

Chapter 1, *Getting Started with Looker*, introduces Looker, a powerful BI tool within the Google Cloud Platform, and guides you through setting up access, connecting data, and building your first visualizations.

Chapter 2, *Configuring Views and Models in a LookML Project* , teaches you how to master the essential components of a Looker project: crafting dimensions and measures in views, joining tables in models, and refining LookML code for optimal data usage.

Chapter 3, *Working with Data in Explores*, teaches you how to design Explores for optimal data presentation, manipulate datasets, merge results, and craft compelling visualizations for informed decision-making.

Chapter 4, *Customizing and Serving Dashboards*, guides you through creating interactive, insightful Looker dashboards that combine visualizations, text, and filters for a comprehensive view of your data.

Chapter 5, *Making Dashboards Interactive through Dynamic Elements*, teaches you to leverage Liquid templating within LookML, creating dynamic links, HTML elements, custom labels, and SQL queries for highly interactive Looker dashboards.

Chapter 6, Troubleshooting Looker, teaches you to diagnose and resolve Looker issues from LookML errors to SQL queries, maintaining a seamless data analytics experience.

Chapter 7, Integrating Looker with Other Applications, explores how Looker seamlessly integrates with external applications such as Google Sheets, Looker Studio, and others, streamlining data workflows and analysis.

Chapter 8, Organizing the Looker Environment, helps you to master Looker content management, including folders, favorites, boards, and Looker Marketplace applications, optimizing navigation and discovery within your Looker instance.

Chapter 9, Administering and Monitoring Looker, empowers you to master Looker administration, covering user management, system monitoring, and advanced settings for optimal control of your data analytics environment.

Chapter 10, Preparing to Develop Looker Applications, introduces you to the tools for building custom applications powered by Looker, exploring APIs, embedding options, the extension framework, components, and the Marketplace.

To get the most out of this book

This book is perfect for beginners – no prior Looker knowledge is needed!

A basic understanding of how data is organized in databases will be helpful but is not necessary.

You'll need a Google account to access Google Cloud and request a Looker trial instance. We'll guide you through the setup process.

Be prepared to learn LookML! This book offers a step-by-step introduction to Looker's data modeling language, helping you build your first models and visualizations.

To access Looker, you don't need to install anything; a web browser is enough.

If you are using the digital version of this book, we advise you to type the code yourself or access the code from the book's GitHub repository (a link is available in the next section). Doing so will help you avoid any potential errors related to the copying and pasting of code.

Download the example code files

You can find the code snippets for this book on GitHub at `https://github.com/PacktPublishing/Business-Intelligence-with-Looker-Cookbook/`. If there's an update to the code, it will be updated in the GitHub repository.

We also have other code bundles from our rich catalog of books and videos available at `https://github.com/PacktPublishing/`. Check them out!

Conventions used

There are a number of text conventions used throughout this book.

`Code in text`: Indicates code words in text, database table names, folder names, filenames, file extensions, pathnames, dummy URLs, user input, and Twitter handles. Here is an example: "If you know what the `WHERE` and `HAVING` commands do in SQL, it is easy to understand the difference between the `sql_always_where` and `sql_always_having` parameters."

A block of code is set as follows:

```
dimension: age_group {
  type: tier
  tiers: [18, 25, 35, 45, 55, 65, 75, 90]
  sql: ${age} ;;
  style: classic
}
```

When we wish to draw your attention to a particular part of a code block, the relevant lines or items are set in bold:

```
<iframe
    src="(add your Embed URL here)"
    width="600"
    height="3600"
    frameborder="0">
</iframe>
```

Bold: Indicates a new term, an important word, or words that you see onscreen. For instance, words in menus or dialog boxes appear in **bold**. Here is an example: "Make sure you are in the Explore environment in the **Orders and Users** Explore."

> **Tips or important notes**
> Appear like this.

Get in touch

Feedback from our readers is always welcome.

General feedback: If you have questions about any aspect of this book, email us at `customercare@packtpub.com` and mention the book title in the subject of your message.

Errata: Although we have taken every care to ensure the accuracy of our content, mistakes do happen. If you have found a mistake in this book, we would be grateful if you would report this to us. Please visit www.packtpub.com/support/errata and fill in the form.

Piracy: If you come across any illegal copies of our works in any form on the internet, we would be grateful if you would provide us with the location address or website name. Please contact us at copyright@packt.com with a link to the material.

If you are interested in becoming an author: If there is a topic that you have expertise in and you are interested in either writing or contributing to a book, please visit authors.packtpub.com.

Share Your Thoughts

Once you've read *Business Intelligence with Looker Cookbook*, we'd love to hear your thoughts! Scan the QR code below to go straight to the Amazon review page for this book and share your feedback.

https://packt.link/r/1-800-56095-8

Your review is important to us and the tech community and will help us make sure we're delivering excellent quality content.

Download a free PDF copy of this book

Thanks for purchasing this book!

Do you like to read on the go but are unable to carry your print books everywhere?

Is your e-book purchase not compatible with the device of your choice?

Don't worry!, Now with every Packt book, you get a DRM-free PDF version of that book at no cost.

Read anywhere, any place, on any device. Search, copy, and paste code from your favorite technical books directly into your application.

The perks don't stop there, you can get exclusive access to discounts, newsletters, and great free content in your inbox daily

Follow these simple steps to get the benefits:

1. Scan the QR code or visit the following link:

https://packt.link/free-ebook/9781800560956

2. Submit your proof of purchase.
3. That's it! We'll send your free PDF and other benefits to your email directly.

1
Getting Started with Looker

"Just as Google's mission is to organize the world's information and make it universally accessible and useful, Looker's is to do the same for your business data so that you can build insight-powered workflows and applications."

This is how the **Welcome to Looker** page greets you. Looker is one of the products of the Google Cloud BI family. The Google Cloud BI family also includes Looker Studio (Free and Pro versions), which was created by Google in 2016 and used to be called Google Data Studio. This book focuses on Looker, and Looker Studio won't be covered.

Looker is an advanced **business intelligence** (**BI**) solution acquired by Google in 2019. It is part of Google Cloud Platform. In order to start using it, you need to fill in the **Contact Sales** form and wait for the free trial to be created for you by someone from the Google Cloud sales team. At the time of writing this book, it is still the process to follow.

You can contact the sales team to get some help with your Looker exploration, but this book aims to make you autonomous in your Looker journey.

In this chapter, we're going to cover the following recipes:

- Getting access to Looker
- Providing access to your team
- Connecting to data in Looker
- Building a LookML project
- Connecting Looker to Git
- Making and saving changes in views
- Creating a LookML model and an Explore
- Building Looks from Explores
- Creating a dashboard from a Look

Technical requirements

In this chapter, we'll be working with the Looker (Google Cloud core), built on Google Cloud infrastructure – therefore, you have nothing to install. You just need internet access, a browser, and a Google (personal or professional) account to access the Google Cloud console.

Getting access to Looker

In this recipe, you will discover how to get access to the Looker environment and start working in it. As mentioned in the introduction, we'll focus on Looker (Google Cloud core), which is available from the Google Cloud console.

How to do it...

The steps for this recipe are as follows:

1. Let's start by going to the Google Cloud website: `https://cloud.google.com/?hl=en`. Once on the website, check whether you're connected with your Gmail account by checking your Gmail profile photo in the top-right corner. Make sure that you're connected with the email account you want to use for your Looker tests. If all is good, in the same top-right corner, click on **Console** (*Figure 1.1*).

Figure 1.1 – Google Cloud home page

2. After clicking on **Console**, you will be redirected to the Google Cloud environment where you will need to choose your country, read and accept the Terms of Service, and click **Agree and Continue**.

3. Note that you might be redirected to a **Console** page in a different language (your local language, for example). To follow the book's guidelines easily, it is preferable to switch to the English version – you can do that in your Google account settings (`https://myaccount.google.com/`) or, on the first Google Cloud page where you clicked on **Console**, there was an option to choose the language before going to the console (check the top-right corner in *Figure 1.1*).

4. If it's your first time working within Google Cloud, you will need to create your first project by clicking on **Create Project** on the right (on the Google Cloud **Welcome** window after clicking on **Agree and Continue**). If you already have projects in your Google Cloud environment, you might still want to create a new one for your Looker experiment.

5. After clicking on **Create Project**, you will need to choose a project name (or keep the default one) and organization, if you have one created – you might have one if you're using your professional account. If not, keep the default **No Organization** option. Click **CREATE** to finalize the project creation (*Figure 1.2*). A Google Cloud project is a way to organize your resources and applications in **Google Cloud Platform** (**GCP**). It is a billing and access control entity. By creating a project, you can group your GCP resources together and control who has access to them. You can always switch between your projects in the top-left corner.

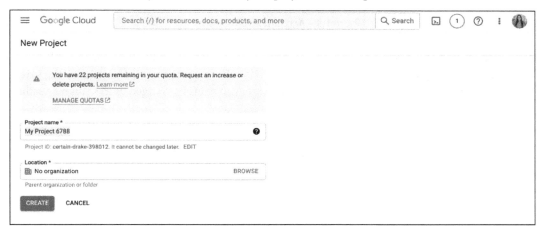

Figure 1.2 – Project creation

6. When you're on the **Welcome** page with your project chosen in the top-left corner, you can continue the activation of your free trial for your **Google Cloud** (**GC**) environment by clicking on **START FREE** in the top-right corner.

7. On the **Step 1 of 2 Account Information** page (*Figure 1.3*), choose your country, and your organization or needs (there is an **Other** option if you don't know yet), and then read and accept the Terms of Service.

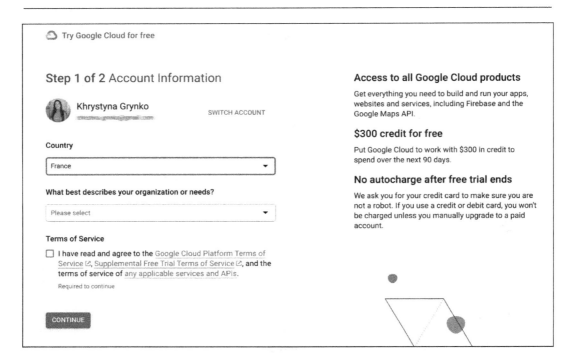

Figure 1.3 – Account information

8. On the **Step 2 of 2** page (*Figure 1.4*), you will need to provide your billing information. There is no autocharge after the free trial ends. Google only asks you for your credit card to make sure you are not a robot. If you use a credit or debit card, you won't be charged unless you manually upgrade to a paid account.

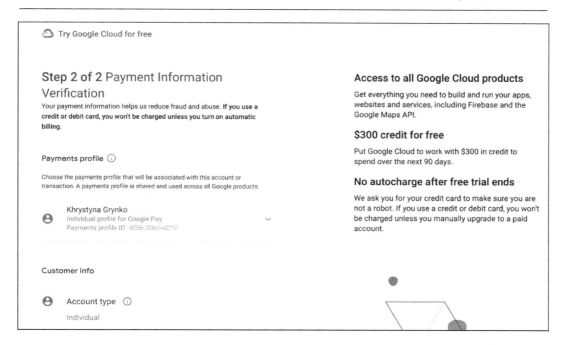

Figure 1.4 – Payment information

9. Google will verify your billing information; this is usually done through your banking application.

10. Now, you'll need to fill in a small questionnaire to help GC serve you better.

11. Let's finally get to Looker! Search for Looker either in the **Search** bar or by clicking on the hamburger button on the left (*Figure 1.5*). You can pin the Looker service in the hamburger menu to have it always at the top of your list.

> **Important note**
>
> Currently, to initiate a Looker free trial within your GC console, you'll need to contact Looker sales directly. You can do this through the following form: https://cloud.google.com/resources/looker-free-trial.

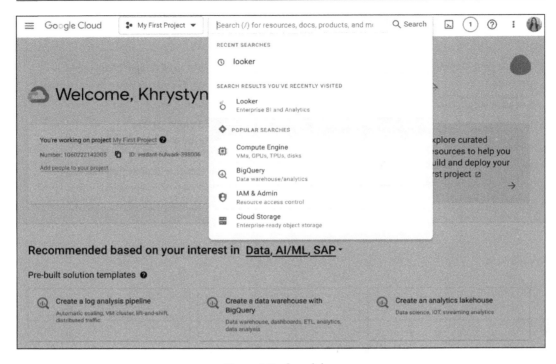

Figure 1.5 – Search bar

12. When you are on the Looker Welcome page, click on CREATE AN INSTANCE (Figure 1.6) to create your Looker instance. Important: To avoid any billing surprises, confirm your free Looker trial is active before creating your instance. You can check the trial status by contacting a Looker sales representative. A Looker instance is a dedicated, isolated environment for running Looker. Looker instances allow users to connect to data sources, model data, explore data, visualize data, share data, and embed analytics.

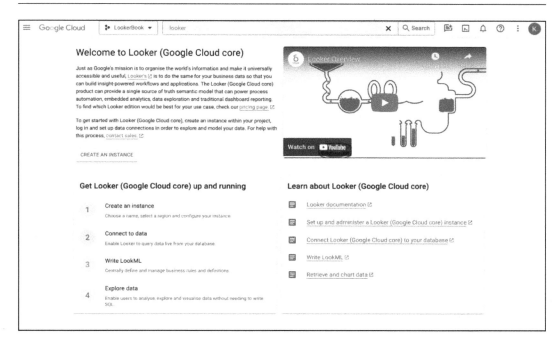

Figure 1.6 – Looker Welcome page

13. If you see a popup that says **Enable required APIs,** click on **Enable.** The Looker (Google Cloud core) API is a RESTful API that allows you to programmatically interact with your Looker instance.

   On the page that will open after you enable the required APIs or after you click on **CREATE AN INSTANCE,** choose your instance name, then add your **OAuth Application Credentials** details to access your instance (*Figure 1.7*). You will need to create your OAuth application credentials in advance. To do this, open a new tab, go to the GC console, click on the menu button in the top - left corner and search for **API & Services** and click on it ->then click on **Credentials** -> then click on **Create credentials** (choose the **Web application** option) -> then choose **OAuth client ID.** It might ask you to create an OAuth consent screen where you will need to provide the app name and your email address in the **Support and Developer** section and keep the default values for the rest.

14. Once your client ID is created, go back to your instance creation form and add your newly created credentials there. Finally, choose a region (if you can't find your country, choose the one that is closer to you geographically) and click **CREATE.** *The creation can take up to 1 hour.*

> **Important note**
>
> After the free trial, your instance may be automatically converted to a paid Looker instance. Please confirm this with your Looker sales representative.

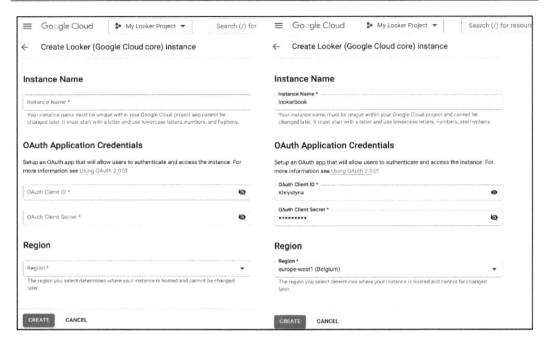

Figure 1.7 – Looker instance creation

15. When the instance is created, you will see your Looker instance link in the **Instance URL** column (*Figure 1.8*).

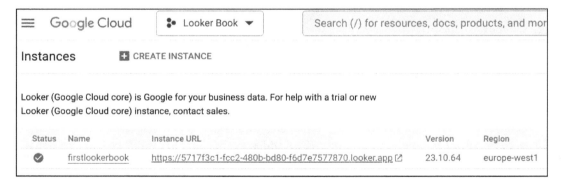

Figure 1.8 – Instance URL

Troubleshooting Instance URL Errors

To avoid getting an error when clicking on the instance URL (such as, for example, **Error 400: redirect_uri_mismatch**), check the following elements:

- You connected with the right Google account (when you're connected with multiple Gmail accounts, the one that is used when you open the instance URL in the new tab might not be the one that has access to your Looker and GC environment)

- In **APIs & Services**, make sure you created your OAuth credentials for the Web application

- In **APIs & Services**, make sure you added your Looker instance URL plus **/oauth2callback** in **Authorized redirect URIs** (*Figure 1.9*)

- In **APIs & Services**, make sure you added **looker.app** as the authorized domain on your OAuth consent screen (click **Edit App** to add it)

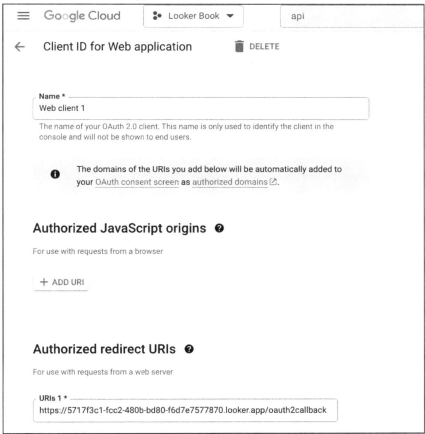

Figure 1.9 – Authorized redirect URIs

There's more...

It is possible to get access to Looker through labs, as a way to test Looker without creating your own GC environment and without setting up a free trial. You can create an account on the Cloud Skills Boost website (https://www.cloudskillsboost.google/) and find free Looker quests and labs (make sure it is Looker and not Looker Studio). The labs on Cloud Skills Boost give you access to the sandbox environment with the data prepared for you. The labs give you a step-by-step exercise and teach you how to use Looker. The inconvenience is that you have limited time for your exercise. Additionally, you cannot work with your data and with your team on one project in the lab. These labs are only for training purposes and give you a good start in understanding the Looker environment.

For more in-depth exploration, you can combine the lab training and this book.

Providing access to your team

When you create your first Looker instance, you become its owner and administrator. You can then provide access to the rest of your team. Remember, by default, with the Standard edition, Looker gives you 12 free user allocations with the Standard version – 2 developers and 10 standard users. The *Standard* edition is tailored for small teams with up to 50 internal platform users.

For your free trial space, it is best to add only the colleagues who will actively participate in testing Looker with you.

How to do it...

To add your colleagues to your Looker free trial instance you will need to do the following:

1. In the GC console, go to the **IAM & Admin** section.
2. Click on the **IAM** tab.
3. Click on **GRANT ACCESS** (*Figure 1.10*).

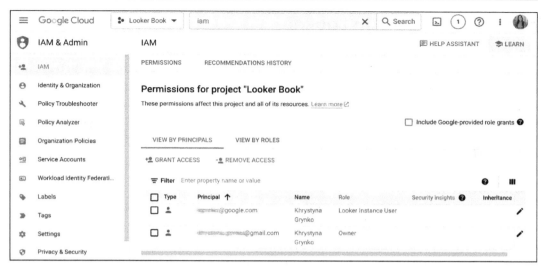

Figure 1.10 – Cloud IAM

4. In **New principals**, add an email (should be a Google account) or multiple emails of your co-testers.

5. In **Select a role**, type `Looker` to filter, then assign your colleagues the same Looker role you have (for example, Looker Admin) to ensure they have the same level of access as you during the trial.

6. Send the Looker instance URL to the person that you provided access to (to find your instance URL, see *Figure 1.8*).

7. When they click on the link or copy and paste it into the browser, they will be asked to authenticate with their Google account.

8. Once authenticated, your colleagues will see the same Looker **Welcome** page you saw when first connected to Looker.

Important note

When managing user permissions in Looker, it's important to grant access based on specific needs. While collaboration is key, admin access should be reserved cautiously. For most colleagues, assigning "Looker instance user" status is sufficient.

See also

- Other (more advanced) user roles and connection options will be discussed later in this book: *Chapter 9, Administering and Monitoring Looker*.

Connecting to data in Looker

You'll need to connect Looker to the data source to start working on your data models, visualizations, and so on. Looker supports over 30 dialects – therefore, it can connect to more than 30 types of databases and data warehouses. The full list of dialects is here: `https://cloud.google.com/looker/docs/looker-core-dialects#supported-dialects-for`. In this book, we will use the connection to BigQuery. BigQuery is Google's fully managed, serverless data warehouse that enables scalable analysis over petabytes of data. BigQuery is quite known as well for its native connection with Google Analytics.

How to do it...

Let's explore BigQuery first. The steps for this are as follows:

1. In your GC console, search for BigQuery in the search bar at the top of the console or in the navigation menu (represented by three horizontal lines) on the left side of the console and you should see your project name in the **Explorer** section (in our case, it's `lookerbook`, but you might have a different name).

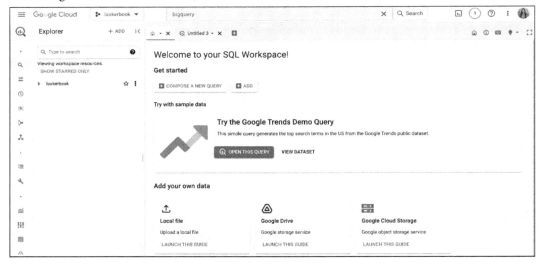

Figure 1.11 – BigQuery welcome page

2. In the **Explorer** section, click on the three dots near your project name (`lookerbook` in the preceding figure) and click on **Create dataset** (*Figure 1.12*). A dataset is like a folder that will contain your future data tables.

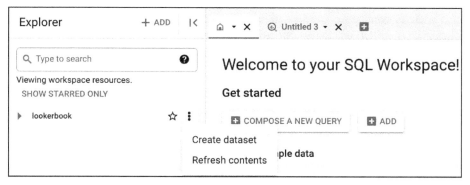

Figure 1.12 – Dataset creation

3. Name your dataset, choose **US** in **Multi-region** where your data will live, and keep everything else as it is, then click on **CREATE DATASET** (*Figure 1.13*).

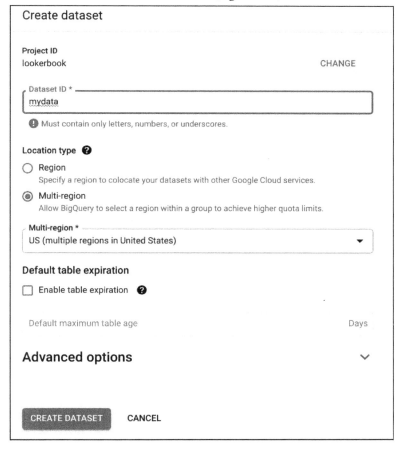

Figure 1.13 – Dataset configurations

4. In this book, to avoid searching for data, we will work with BigQuery public datasets. BigQuery public datasets are datasets that are stored in BigQuery and made available to the general public through the Google Cloud Public Dataset Program. These datasets are provided by a variety of organizations, including government agencies, non-profit organizations, and businesses. You can load your own data into BigQuery (for example, click on three dots near your newly created dataset, click on **Create table**, and then **Create table from**). For more information on how to load your data into BigQuery, check this link: `https://cloud.google.com/bigquery/docs/loading-data`.

5. To work with the public dataset, you first need to add it to your **Explorer** section (to make it visible). The public dataset is not stored in your project; it is hosted by Google, so you won't have to pay for storage. But you can create the table out of the public dataset table to store it in your project.

6. To add the public dataset to your BigQuery space, click on **ADD** in your **Explorer** section, then click on **Star a project by name** (*Figure 1.14*) and add `bigquery-public-data`.

7. Another option to add public datasets is to go to **Additional sources** in *Figure 1.14*, and from there, you can scroll to find public datasets.

8. You can then explore the different datasets available and click **View dataset** when there is one you find interesting – usually, after that, you will see the `bigquery-public-data` project pinned in **Explorer** with all the datasets in it.

Figure 1.14 – Adding a public dataset

9. Find the **Google Analytics 4** (**GA4**) dataset in your starred `bigquery-public-data` project. It is not real GA4 data but it will give you an idea of how your GA4 data will look in BigQuery. Click on `ga4_obfuscated_sample_ecommerce` and then click on the `events_(92)` table (using the **SCHEMA**, **DETAILS**, and **PREVIEW** tabs in *Figure 1.15*).

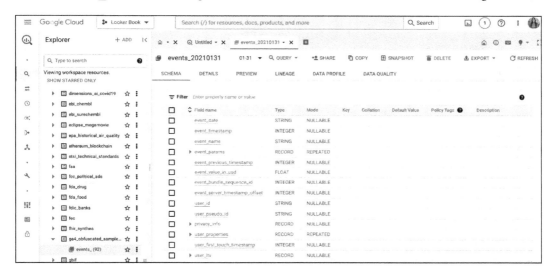

Figure 1.15 – Google Analytics dataset

10. Click on QUERY button (located above the SCHEMA, DETAILS and other table-related tabs), then choose **In new tab**, enter the following SQL query, then click RUN (*Figure1.16*):

```sql
SELECT
PARSE_DATE("%Y%m%d",event_date) as Session_Date,
device.category AS Device_category,
COUNT(*) AS Nb_of_sessions
FROM
   `bigquery-public-data.ga4_obfuscated_sample_ecommerce.
   events_202101*`
WHERE event_name = 'session_start'
GROUP BY 1,2
ORDER BY 1,2 ASC;
```

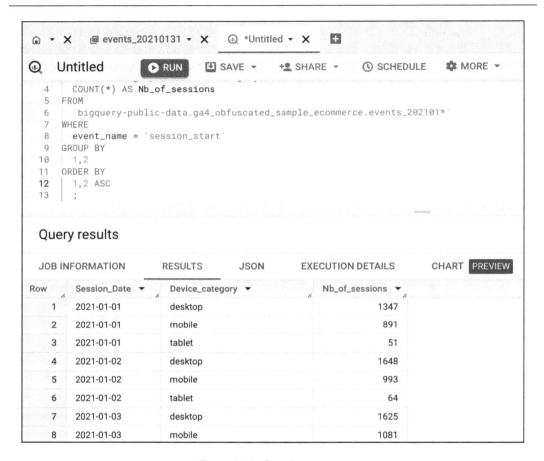

Figure 1.16 – Running a query

11. In this query, we're trying to get the number of sessions on the website per device type by day for January 2021. Click on **SAVE RESULTS** above your **Query results** table and save it as **BigQuery table** (*Figure 1.17*) to your previously created dataset (mydata or another name if you decided to name it differently) in your GC project.

12. Name the table `device_category_jan2021` and then click **Export**.

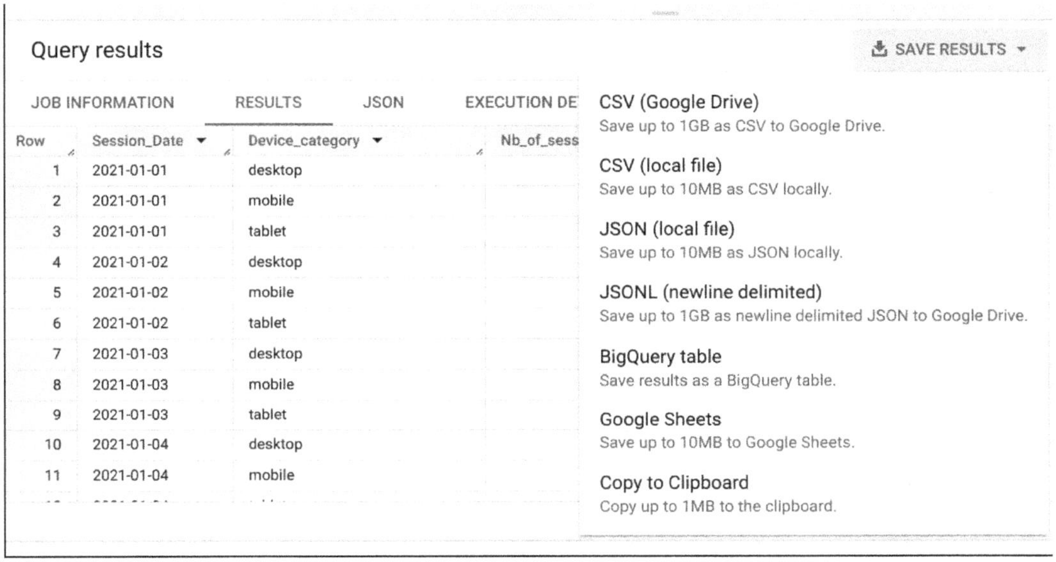

Figure 1.17 – Save the results

13. If you see that the job (all tasks are called jobs in BigQuery) failed, it might be because your dataset was created in another region. Getting a table from the public dataset that is in **US** and exporting it to your dataset in **EU** is not possible, so make sure that you created your `mydata` dataset in the **US** multi-region.

14. Go and check whether the table was created. Now, you have your own dataset that contains your own small table (*Figure 1.18*).

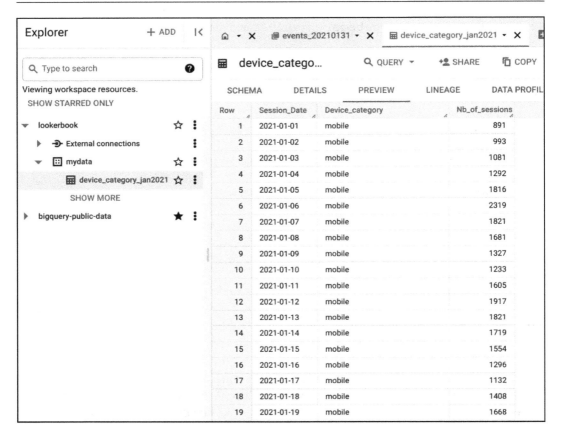

Figure 1.18 – Device category table

Connecting Looker to BigQuery

Let's go back to our Looker instance to connect Looker to BigQuery. Make sure you have at least two tabs open – one with the GC console and another one with the Looker instance.

Let's explore the Looker environment. The steps for this are as follows:

1. In your Looker instance, click on **Admin** on the left, then click on **Database** and **Connections**, and then click the **Add Connection** button (*Figure 1.19*).

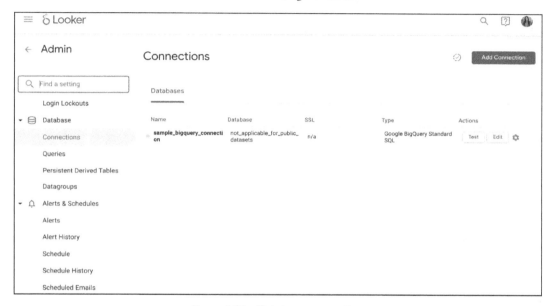

Figure 1.19 – Database connection

2. When you click on **Add Connection**, give your connection a name (`bq_connection1`, in our case) and choose a dialect (**Google BigQuery Standard SQL** in our case).

3. Fill in the form (*Figure 1.20*) with your billing project ID and dataset, choose the standard UTC time zone, and for the rest, keep the default values, then click on CONNECT to establish the connection. To find your project ID (where the billing is configured), go to the GC console, click on your project name in the top-left corner near the Google Cloud logo, and copy the ID from the pop-up window.

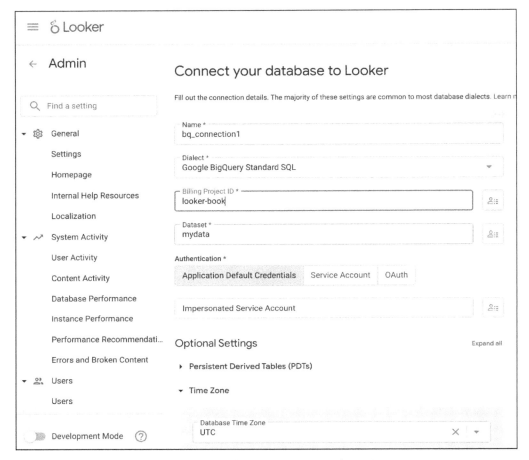

Figure 1.20 – Database connection configuration

How it works...

The connection was relatively simple because Looker (Google Cloud core) has a native connection with GC services. We also configured very few elements, to keep it simple. The goal of this chapter is to quickly go through the Looker basics to give you an overview of how it works. Let's continue with the LookML project creation.

See also

- Connecting Looker to your database: `https://cloud.google.com/looker/docs/looker-core-dialects`

- About BigQuery: `https://cloud.google.com/bigquery?hl=en`

Building a LookML project

A LookML project is a collection of LookML files that describe how to access and model data for BI and data visualization.

Think of LookML as a collection of recipe instructions for turning raw data into insightful dishes. Instead of ingredients and steps, you define the data's components (such as customer names, product types, and sales numbers) and how to combine them (think filtering, grouping, and calculating). Looker, your helpful kitchen assistant, reads these instructions and provides the data ready to be used by anyone, no matter their data-cooking skills.

LookML files are written in a declarative language that defines the dimensions, measures, calculations, and relationships between tables in a database. Looker uses LookML to generate SQL queries that retrieve data from the database and present it in a user-friendly interface. The key components of a LookML project are model files, view files, Explores, dimensions and measures. LookML projects are a powerful way to create a single source of truth for your data.

Getting ready

Before creating your first LookML project, make sure **Development Mode** is activated (*Figure 1.21*). To do this, in the left navigation panel, toggle the **Development Mode** switch on.

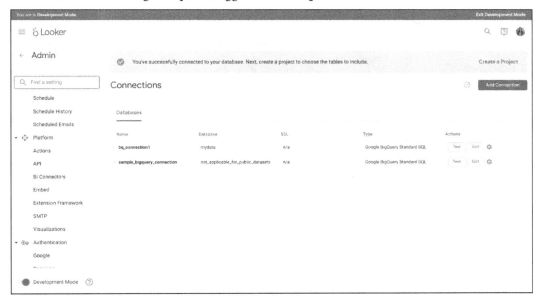

Figure 1.21 – Development Mode toggle

You can exit **Development Mode** by clicking on **Exit Development Mode** in the top-right corner.

In the next chapters, we will work with **Development Mode** activated.

How to do it...

The steps for this recipe are as follows:

1. Exit from the **Admin** navigation tab and make sure you see the **Explore**, **Develop**, and **Admin** tabs on the left.

2. Click on **Develop**, then click on **Projects** (*Figure 1.22*).

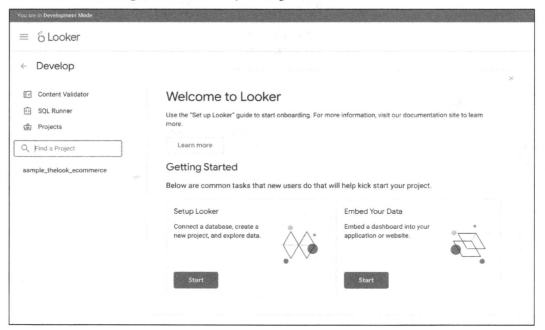

Figure 1.22 – Projects

3. When you're on the **Projects** page, click on **New LookML project**.

4. On the project creation page, give your project a name (test_project in our case), choose the database/data warehouse connection you created previously (bq_connection1), keep the other fields as they are, and click on **Create Project** (*Figure 1.23*).

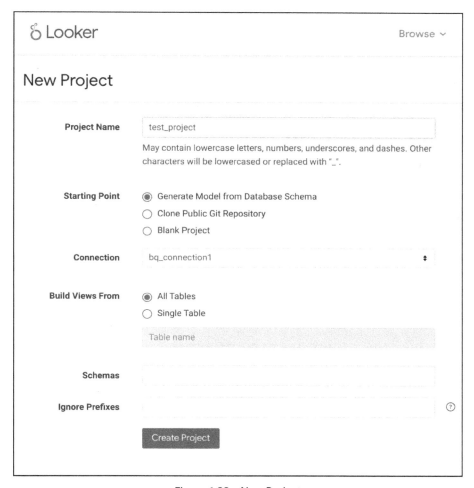

Figure 1.23 – New Project

5. In some cases, you might want to create multiple LookML projects. For example, LookML projects can have multiple model files, but if you want to set different permissions for users to view and edit LookML for specific model files, you can create separate projects for each model.

How it works...

When creating your LookML project, you have three starting points available:

The **Generate Model from DB Schema** option is the one we used in this chapter; it gives Looker the possibility to automatically detect tables and table columns and build a basic model that you can edit if you need to. It is an option that is used quite often.

For some specific cases, you might want to create a blank project to start everything from scratch. To do this, select **Blank Project**.

When you choose **Clone Public Git Repository**, you can get some LookML models, views, and other files configured and ready to use from the existing Git repository.

In this chapter, we chose the first option. But even this option eventually needs a Git connection so you can work on your LookML projects with your colleagues and/or partners and have certain version control in case there are any changes made.

When you create your first project, you will see the LookML development page with an automatically created model and view (or views, depending on whether you have one or multiple tables) – see *Figure 1.24*.

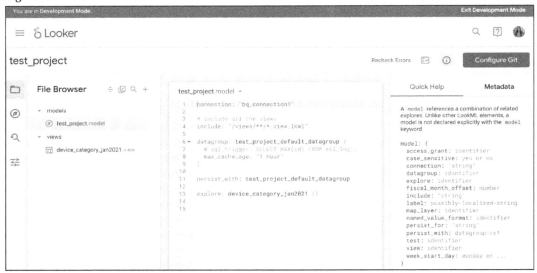

Figure 1.24 – LookML model and view

See also

- Introduction to LookML: https://cloud.google.com/looker/docs/what-is-lookml

Connecting Looker to Git

LookML projects are version-controlled using Git, which allows LookML developers to track changes, collaborate on the project, see the history, revert to previous versions, and configure CI/CD.

Getting ready

Make sure you are on your LookML project (*Figure 1.24*). To get to your LookML environment, you can click on the menu on the left (the **Explore**, **Develop**, and **Admin** tabs), then click on **Develop** and choose your project (`test_project` in our case).

How to do it...

The steps for this recipe are as follows:

1. On your LookML page, click on **Configure Git** in the upper right-hand corner of the page (almost any Git provider will work, including GitHub, GitLab, and Bitbucket).

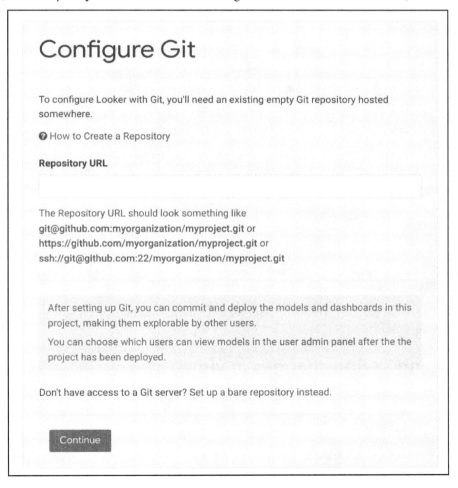

Figure 1.25 – Configure Git

2. If you don't yet have a Git repository where you want your LookML project to live, you can click on **Set up a bare repository instead** (*Figure 1.25*).

> **Important note**
>
> For secure and reliable version control, consider using your own Git repository hosted outside of your Looker server. This ensures that your LookML code and its history are safe, even if something happens to the Looker instance or server.

3. On the **Configure Bare Git Repository** page, click on **Create Repository**.

4. After clicking on **Create Repository**, click on **Back to project**.

How it works...

Once your LookML project is connected to Git, you can start tracking changes to your files. Any changes you make will be saved to your local Git branch. When you are ready to share your changes with other developers, you can push your branch to the remote repository.

Other developers can then pull your changes to their local branches and merge them into their own work. If there are any conflicts, Git will help you to resolve them.

When you are ready to deploy your changes to production, you can merge your development branch into the production branch. Looker will then automatically deploy the latest changes to your production environment.

There's more...

You can use your existing Git repository for Looker. For this, provide your repository URL on the **Configure Git** page (*Figure 1.25*). You can create a new repository on one of the supported Git platforms: GitHub, GitLab, Bitbucket, Phabricator Diffusion and others.

On the **Configure Git** page (*Figure 1.25*), there are links to the instructions on how to create your repository in any of the listed Git platforms.

Making and saving changes in views

Views in Looker are tables of data that are defined in LookML. Views can be based on existing database tables, or they can be derived from tables that are created using LookML-based query or SQL query.

Views are used to organize data in Looker. They can also be used to create custom dimensions and measures. Views are typically declared in view files, with one view per file. Each view file contains a definition of the table, including the fields that are included in the view.

Views can be used in Explores to create data visualizations. They can also be used in joins to combine data from multiple views.

Getting ready

Make sure you are in **Development Mode**. Go to your LookML project environment and, on the left, open the views section/list. At this stage, you should see only one view based on the table we have in our BigQuery dataset – `device_category_jan2021`. Select this view to see the view's LookML code in the code editor in the middle of the page (*Figure 1.26*).

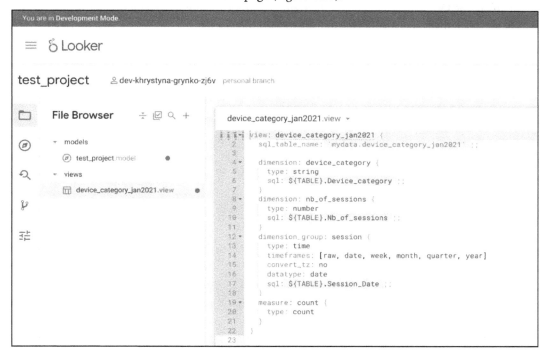

Figure 1.26 – The device_category view

We will make small changes in the views to see how the LookML code works and how you can prepare your data in this Looker semantic layer for your users.

How to do it...

The steps for this recipe are as follows:

1. Place the cursor after line 6 (`sql: ${TABLE}.Device_category ;;`) and press *Enter* on your keyboard. In Looker, there's a special character – $ – that acts as a substitution operator. It's used to create more reusable and modular LookML code, allowing you to reference elements that have already been defined within your code. This helps to make your code cleaner, more organized, and easier to maintain.

2. Explore the **Quick Help** section on the right that proposes different elements that you can add to enrich, enhance, or complete your dimension (*Figure 1.27*).

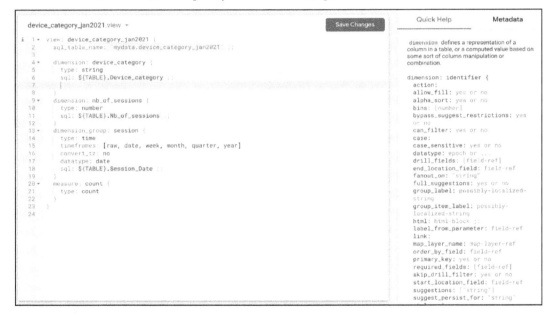

Figure 1.27 – Quick Help

3. In the empty line, start typing the word `description`, then add a description similar or different to the one in *Figure 1.28*.

Figure 1.28 – Dimension description

4.   Place the cursor after line 21 (type: count) and press *Enter* on your keyboard.

5.   In the empty line, start typing the word description, then add a description similar or different to the one in *Figure 1.29*.

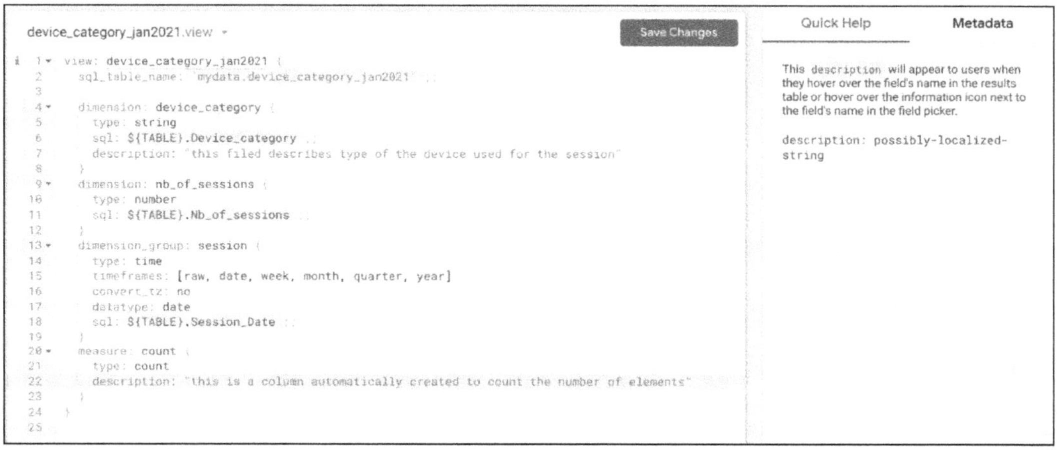

Figure 1.29 – Measure description

6.   Place your cursor on line 23 after the curly bracket and press *Enter*. You can now start creating new measures. Copy and paste this code to create a new measure that will count the total of sessions (per device, per day, depending on the dimensions that you will choose for your visualization later):

```
measure: total_sessions {
  type: sum
  sql: ${nb_of_sessions} ;;
}
```

7.   Now that we have added some descriptions and created a new measure, we want to make sure that our code is correct. To do this, you should click on **Save Changes**, then click on **Validate LookML** in the top-right corner (*Figure 1.30*). If everything is correct, you will see **No LookML errors found** in the **Project Health** window on the right.

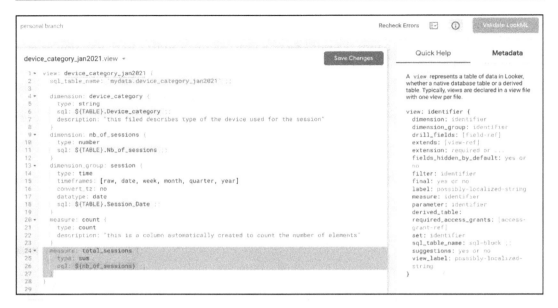

Figure 1.30 – Validate LookML

8.   Click on **Save Changes**.

9.   You will now see the **Commit Changes and Push** button in the top-right corner; you might want to use it when you are ready to share your work with your teammates (if you don't push changes to your Git repository, your team won't be able to see your LookML project and the changes made to it). Don't rush to commit. Verify your LookML edits by testing them in an Explore before committing permanently (Explores will be explained in the next recipe).

How it works...

As explained previously, a view is a representation of a table in LookML that contains dimensions and measures that are used to define the data that can be used in Explores to create data visualizations.

In Looker, dimensions are filterable data columns (like dates, names, IDs) that often come from your tables, but some can be built within LookML. For example, device_category and session_date are different dimensions within our BigQuery dataset.

Measures are aggregations of one or more dimensions (or unique attributes of the data) such as a count or average. Measures allow you to calculate key performance indicators (KPIs) that help your users analyze data using different aggregated attributes.

Once the view or the views are created, and all the necessary dimensions and metrics are enriched/completed/added, you can save changes and use your views in models and Explores.

See also

- For a more in-depth exploration of the views and models, please refer to the following chapter: *Chapter 2, Configuring Views and Models in a LookML Project*

- Views in Looker: `https://cloud.google.com/looker/docs/reference/param-view-view`

- Incorporating SQL and referring to LookML objects (the $ substitution operator, etc.): `https://cloud.google.com/looker/docs/sql-and-referring-to-lookml`

Creating a LookML model and Explore

As seen in the previous recipe, a LookML project is a collection of files that define a semantic data model for a SQL database. It contains model files, view files, and other types of files. We explored views that represent your database/data warehouse tables. Now, to make these dimensions and measures in the views usable, we need to create Explores.

An **Explore** is a custom view of the data that is defined using a LookML model. It is the starting point for querying data in Looker. Explores in Looker empower self-service data analysis with secure access, enabling creation of reports, dashboards, and visualizations. Explores can be based on one or multiple tables.

Explores are created in the LookML model file. The LookML model files contain Explores based on one or multiple tables joined (*Figure 1.31*).

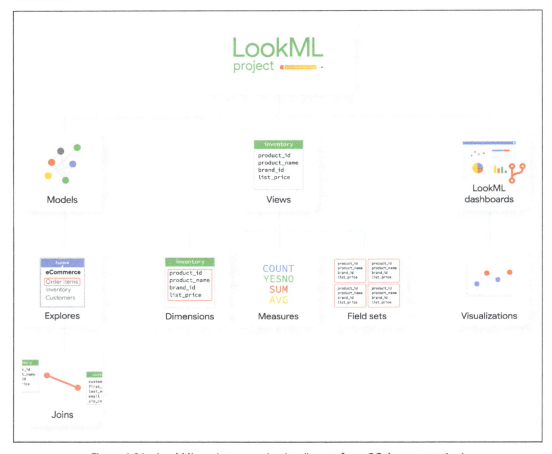

Figure 1.31 – LookML project organization (image from GC documentation)

Model files can contain different additional parameters, which we will review later in this book.

Getting ready

When you created your LookML projects and chose **Generate Model from Database Schema**, your model file was created by default. Click on your `test_project.model` model file to open it in the code editor (*Figure 1.32*). In this model file created automatically, you see multiple elements: `connection`, `include`, `datagroup`, `persist_with`, and `explore`. We will understand the meaning of all of them later, but for now, let's create our own model file and the Explore in it.

Make sure you're in **Development Mode**.

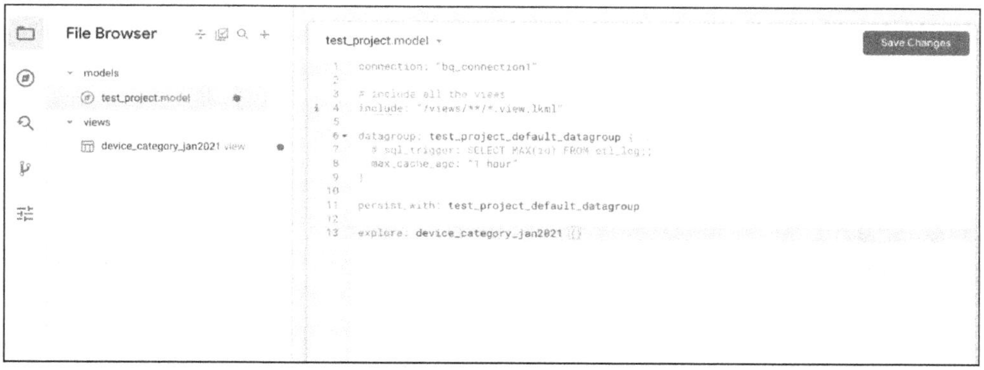

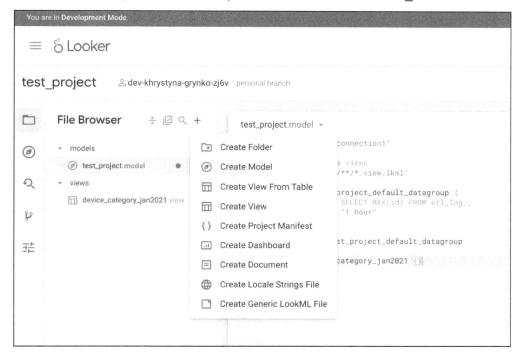

Figure 1.32 – Model

How to do it...

The steps for this recipe are as follows:

1. To the right of **File Browser**, click on the + symbol and choose **Create Model** (*Figure 1.33*). You will need to provide a name for your model; let's call it `devices_model`.

Figure 1.33 – LookML file creation

2. When the model file is created, it is usually created outside of the **models** section but you can always move it there (just drag and drop it). You will see that the model contains `connection` and `include` sample elements. `connection` specifies the database/data warehouse connection, and `include` specifies the files that can be used in this model. You can change these elements if needed, but for now, we'll keep the default options. Other elements are commented with the # symbol, and serve to show you how to create your first Explores based on multiple views (*Figure 1.34*).

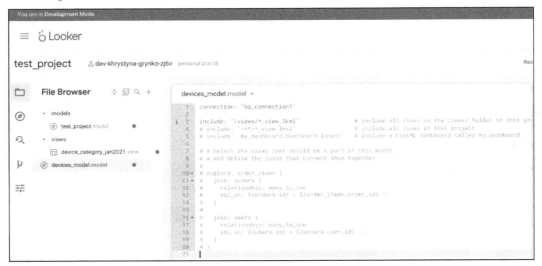

Figure 1.34 – Device model

3. Delete all the commented (gray) section and start typing `explore: {}`. Add the name of our only view, `device_category_jan2021`. It will look like this: `explore: 'device_category_jan2021 {}'` (*Figure 1.35*). It is something we've seen in the automatically created model. The `include` parameter that you see in the figure is a way to bring together different LookML files. It lets you access and use components from other files within your current file. You can use it in `model`, `view`, and `explore` files to include different types of files, such as view files, dashboard files, Explore files, and data test files.

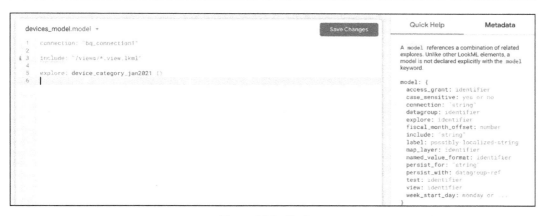

Figure 1.35 – Explore

4. Click on **Save Changes**.

5. Click on the arrow icon to the right of devices_model.model and make sure that Explore Device Category Jan2021 - devices_model was created (*Figure 1.36*).

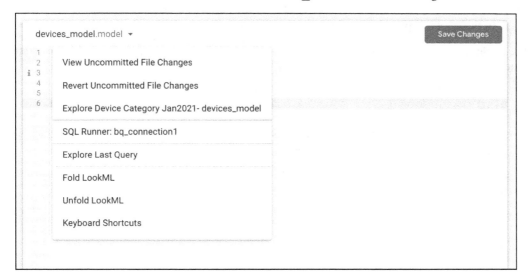

Figure 1.36 – Model drop-down list

6. Click on Explore Device Category Jan2021 - devices_model and the **Explore** environment will open (*Figure 1.37*).

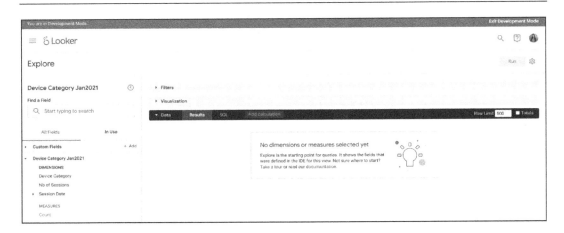

Figure 1.37 – Explore environment

How it works...

Looker has three basic types of users: **Developer** (**Admin**), **Standard** (**Creator**), and **Viewer**. When we were in the LookML project, we acted as a **Developer** user.

In the **Explore** space that we just opened, we'll act as **Standard** users or creators, those who can create visualizations (or Looks). Let's explore Explores in the next sections.

See also

- For a more in-depth exploration of the views and models, please refer to the following chapter: *Chapter 2, Configuring Views and Models in a LookML Project*
- For a more in-depth exploration of the Explores, please refer to the following chapter: *Chapter 3, Working with Data in Explores*
- Looker model files: https://cloud.google.com/looker/docs/lookml-project-files#model_files
- Explore in Looker: https://cloud.google.com/looker/docs/reference/param-explore-explore

Building visualizations (Looks) from Explores

Explores are built by developers for creators so that creators don't have to think about how to prepare the data, join tables, specify cache and so on. All they should do is choose their columns, and visualization types, add filters if needed, and save their work.

Looks are individual data visualizations or tables based on Explores that can be readily integrated into dashboards. Edits to a Look automatically update in all dashboards where it's included, ensuring consistent and accurate data. Note that it's uncommon to save everything as a single Look and then add it to a dashboard. This approach makes folder organization difficult. Usually, you create a visualization within Explore and save it to a dashboard directly from Explore.

Getting ready

Make sure you are in the **Explore** environment (*Figure 1.37*). On the left, you have the columns available. They can be from one (in our case) or multiple tables joined. In the middle, you have three sections: **Filters**, **Visualization**, and **Data**. In the top-right corner, you have the *gear* icon and **Run** button. We're currently in the Explore called **Device Category Jan2021**.

Let's build our first Look.

How to do it...

The steps for this recipe are as follows:

1. Make sure your columns are visible by clicking on the arrow to the right of **Device Category Jan2021** to expand the list of columns (a field picker) in the left panel.

2. Click on the **Device Category** column and you will see it appear in the **Results** panel in the middle of the screen (*Figure 1.38*).

3. Expand the **Session Date** list of columns in the right panel and click on **Date**.

4. Then, click on **Nb of Sessions**, and in the top-right corner, click on **Run** to send the request to your BigQuery data warehouse. You will then obtain the table with the results (*Figure 1.38*).

Figure 1.38 – Query results

5. Expand the **Visualization** section by clicking on it. The visualization you'll see probably will not make any sense; we'll work on our columns and visualization to show something meaningful.

6. At this stage, our **Nb of Sessions** column is located in **DIMENSIONS** and not **MEASURES** so Looker probably doesn't read it as quantitative data. If you click on the three dots near your **Nb of Sessions** column, you will see available options to modify the column. Click on **Aggregate** and then on **Sum** (*Figure 1.39*). This will create a custom field called Sum of Nb of Sessions. While Looker developers typically fill the field picker by creating dimensions and measures in the LookML project, custom fields let you create your own dimensions and measures in Explores. Custom fields you add won't be saved permanently within the data model.

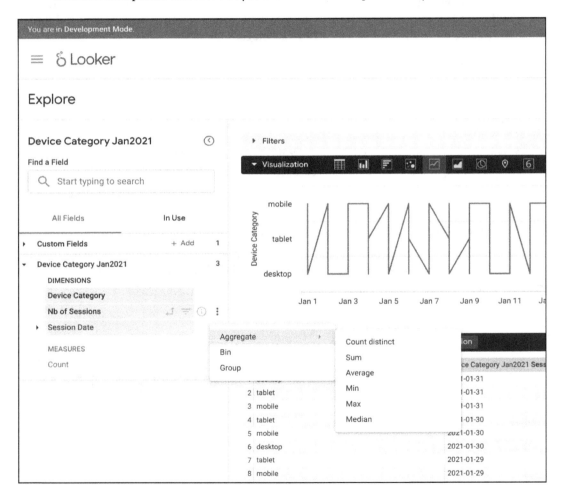

Figure 1.39 – Dimension to measure

7. Let's restart our Look (visualization) creation by first removing the columns we chose before. Click on the *gear* icon near your column name in the **Results** section, then click on **Remove** (*Figure 1.40*).

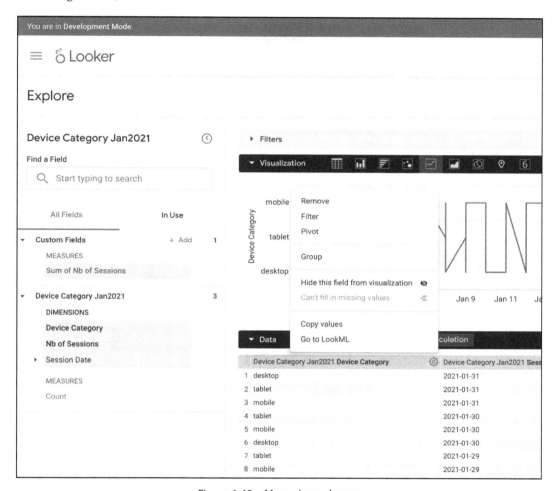

Figure 1.40 – Managing columns

8. Once you have cleaned the **Results** table by removing the columns, click on the **Device Category** and **Sum of Nb of Sessions** columns in your left panel to make them appear in the **Results** table, and click on **Run** to populate the data.

9. Once the data is there, in the **Visualization** panel in the **Column** visualization (the second icon after the word *Visualization*), you will see a column chart visualization appear on your screen (*Figure 1.41*).

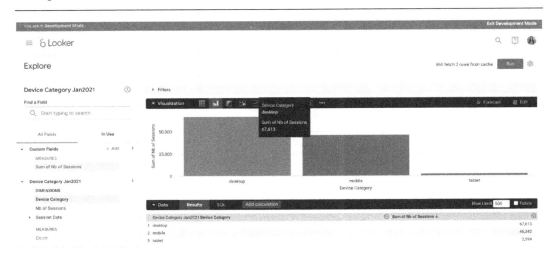

Figure 1.41 – Visualization

10. Click on the *gear* icon near the **Run** button and choose **Save…** and **As a Look** (*Figure 1.42*). Give it the name Nb of Sessions per Device and click on **Save**.

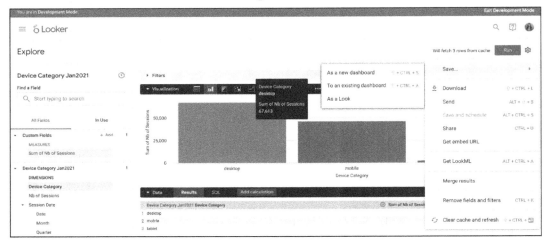

Figure 1.42 – Managing the created Look

11. Now, let's create another visualization (Look). Remove **Device Category** from the **Results** panel and click on **Session Date** and then **Date**. Our goal here is to see the evolution of the number of sessions per day. Once you have your two columns, **Date** and **Sum Nb of Sessions**, click on **Run.**

12. In the **Visualization** panel, choose the **Line** visualization and you will see the evolution of the number of sessions per day in your graphic (*Figure 1.43*). *As a reminder, sessions = visits to the website.*

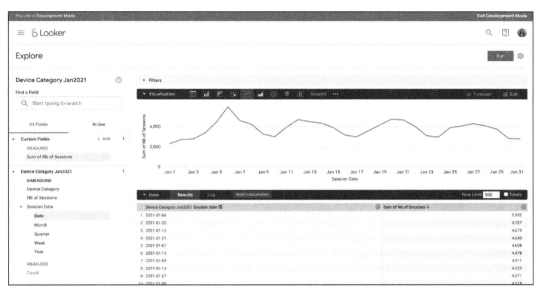

Figure 1.43 – Line visualization

13. Save this visualization as a Look with the title Nb of Sessions per Day.

14. Go to the home page (by clicking on the Looker logo in the top-left corner).

15. Click on **Folders** and then **My folder** in the left panel (*Figure 1.44*) to verify that your Looks were created.

Figure 1.44 – Folders

How it works...

Explores are usually created by the LookML developers (data engineers, Looker admin, and so on) so that analysts can build their dashboards using the available prepared columns in the **Explore** space. In this recipe, we created Looks (visualizations) from the columns that were available thanks to the work that has been done in the LookML space. Every time we choose a combination of columns and click **Run**, Looker, in the backend, launches an SQL query to our database or data warehouse. The way Looker connects to the data, reads the data, does the joins, and so on – all that is specified in our LookML project.

Creating a dashboard from a Look

After you have learned how to explore and visualize data, you can start creating dashboards. Dashboards let you put multiple tables or graphs on one page so you can quickly see related information. You can also make dashboards interactive so users can filter them down to the specific data they want.

How to do it...

The steps for this recipe are as follows:

1. On the Looker home page, click on **Folders**.
2. In **My folder** (where you have a list of Looks you created), open the **Nb of Sessions per Day** Look by clicking on it.
3. In the **Nb of Sessions per Day** Look, click on the *gear* icon in the top-right corner and click **Save...** and then **As a new dashboard** (*Figure 1.45*). Give your new dashboard a name, `Sessions Dashboard`, and click **Save**.

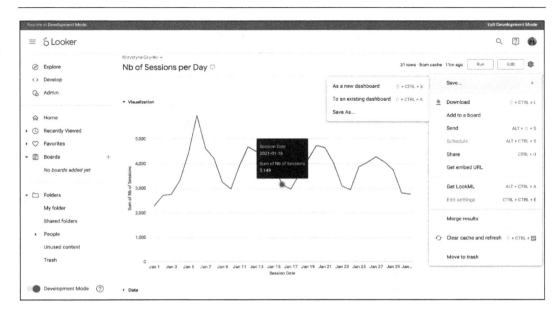

Figure 1.45 – Saving as a new dashboard

4. Go back to **Folders** followed by **My folder** to check whether the dashboard was created (*Figure 1.46*).

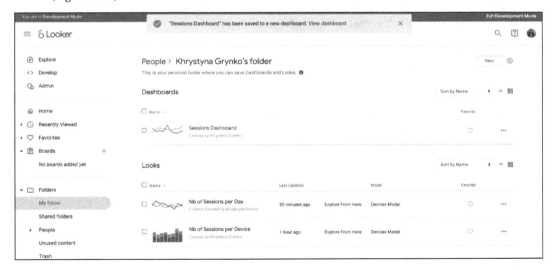

Figure 1.46 – My folder: Dashboard and Looks

5. Click on the **Nb of Sessions per Device** Look, then once in the Look, click on the **gear icon** in the top-right corner, click **Save** and **To an existing dashboard**, and then choose the dashboard you created in the previous steps, **Sessions Dashboard**. Click **Save to Dashboard**.

6. In the green ribbon that appears after you click on **Save to Dashboard**, click on **Sessions Dashboard** (*Figure 1.47*) to check your dashboard and whether all the Looks were added.

Figure 1.47 – Dashboard creation message

A dashboard can contain more than two Looks. In this recipe, we explored a simple dashboard to understand how it works, but we'll dive deeper into this topic later in this book.

How it works...

In this recipe, we created the dashboard from a Look. Note that Look should be in the same folder with the dashboard. There are multiple other ways to create dashboards in Looker, as follows:

*   Create an empty dashboard and then build Looks through the **Explore** interface in the dashboard (click **Add** in the top-left corner of the dashboard)

*   Create a dashboard from the LookML dashboard file

*   Create a dashboard through the Looker API

See also

*   *Chapter 4, Customizing and Serving the Dashboards*

*   *Chapter 5, Making Dashboards Interactive through Dynamic Elements*

*   Looker dashboards: https://cloud.google.com/looker/docs/dashboards

2
Configuring Views and Models in a LookML Project

As discussed in the previous chapter, the key components of a **LookML** project are model files and view files. Views contain dimensions and measures that represent the columns in the tables. One view equals one table (or a virtual table known as a database or data warehouse view). In the views, you can define the fields (dimensions and measures) that are available to users from each table, specify the labels and descriptions for each field, set default values for filters and other parameters, define custom calculations for measures, filter, and sort the data.

LookML model files are the foundation of any Looker application. They define the data that users can access and explore. By carefully designing your LookML model files, you can make it easy for users to find the data they need and to get the insights they need to make informed decisions. In LookML models, you can create the Explores based on one or multiple tables (views).

When you create your LookML project, and if you choose **Generate Model** from **Database Schema** and then **All Tables**, Looker will try to create the views and the model for you. But you will certainly need to make some modifications to prepare the data to be used by users in the Explore environment. You might also choose to create a blank project or clone an existing GitHub repository with the LookML code.

In this chapter, we will learn how you can prepare your data in views and, when it's ready and complete, create the Explores in the model with the proper configuration.

In this chapter, we're going to cover the following recipes:

- Creating dimensions in views
- Creating measures in views
- Describing data in LookML views
- Working with filters in LookML views
- Joining tables in models

- Adding advanced model parameters
- Working with LookML files
- Working with geodata in LookML
- Reusing the LookML code

> **Note**
>
> Do kindly note that some recipes in this chapter might be a little advanced. These include the following: *Adding advanced model parameters, Working with LookML files, Working with geodata in LookML,* and *Reusing the LookML code.* Consider trying these once you feel more comfortable using Looker!

Technical requirements

The preparation work for this chapter consists of the following steps:

1. In your BigQuery environment in the `bigquery-public-data` list, scroll to find **thelook_ecommerce dataset** (`https://console.cloud.google.com/marketplace/product/bigquery-public-data/thelook-ecommerce`) (*Figure 2.1*).

2. Click on **Copy** in the top-right of the window above the dataset description (*Figure 2.1*).

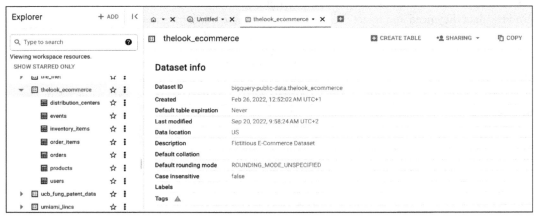

Figure 2.1 – BigQuery dataset

3. Click **Create** to create a new dataset that will 'receive' the copy of **thelook_ecommerce** dataset. Give your future dataset a name (it can be the exact same name - **thelook_ecommerce**, choose **US multiregion**, and create the dataset. You might be requested to activate the Data Transfer API.

4. Once the dataset is copied to your newly created dataset, you will see it appear under your project name in the BigQuery Explorer (*Figure 2.2*).

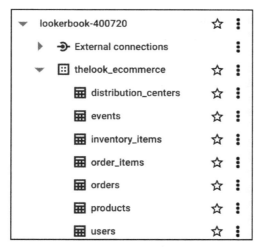

Figure 2.2 – BigQuery tables

The dataset we just copied is a fictitious e-commerce dataset (`https://console.cloud.google.com/marketplace/product/bigquery-public-data/thelook-ecommerce`), which will help us to work on one of the most popular use cases in data analytics – exploring the e-commerce data.

5. Now, we need to connect Looker to this newly created dataset by creating a new database connection in the Looker admin section (Looker menu button -> Admin -> Database -> Connections). Let's call the connection lb_thelookecommerce (*Figure 2.3*).

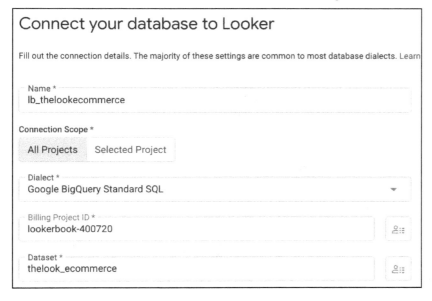

Figure 2.3 – Database/data warehouse connection

6. With our newly created data connection, we can create the new LookML project: **Looker menu button -> Develop -> Projects, on the Projects page click on New LookML Project.**. Name it LB_ecommerce or lb_thelook_ecommerce (or any other name) and keep other fields untouched (*Figure 2.4*).

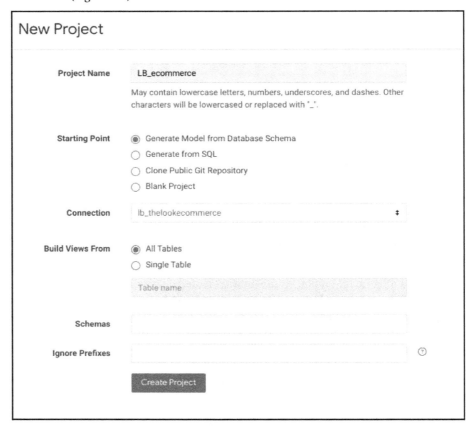

Figure 2.4 – LookML project creation

Now that everything is ready, we can start working on our views and model in the LookML environment. When you choose **Generate Model** from Database Schema during the LookML project creation, Looker automatically creates views that correspond to your tables and the model.

You will see the automatically created Explores in the model, based on one or multiple joined views – Looker creates joins based on naming convention (for example, users.id = orders.user_id), but you might want to recreate these joins later to make sure they fit your data use cases. The joins are used to join multiple tables together; for example, they are used to join the Users table with the Orders table in order to analyze the number of orders per user.

The created Explores will help us to verify our modified dimensions on the real data.

Let's see how it works.

Creating dimensions in views

When you create your LookML project and choose **Generate Model** from **Database Schema**, Looker detects the views (`tables`) and the view fields (`columns`) automatically. It usually adds three parameters to every column: name (`dimension:`), data type (`time`, `string`, `number`, `yes/no`, `tier`, `date`, etc.), and SQL (by default, it references the table and the name of the column in this table); `${field_name}` references a specific field within a LookML file. Sometimes, Looker adds a `primary_key` parameter, if it detects a field that can be potentially a primary key field; it is important for join operations (many to many, many to one, one to many, etc.). By default, Looker creates all the fields (columns) as dimensions (qualitative data) and adds some measures.

Our job is to enrich and complete this data by adding the parameters to our existing dimensions and measures, and by creating new dimensions and measures.

How do we know what is needed? It is something to do before the Looker configuration. We need to understand how Looker will be used, by whom, for what, and so on. We need to define data use cases to make sure we cover them when preparing our data in LookML.

Getting ready

In this section, we will learn to modify our existing dimensions or create new ones. The number of parameters that can be added to the dimensions in Looker is large. For example, if you click on the `users.view` and click *Enter* after the SQL line, you will see on your right, in the **Quick Help** section, multiple parameters that can be added to your dimension (*Figure 2.5*).

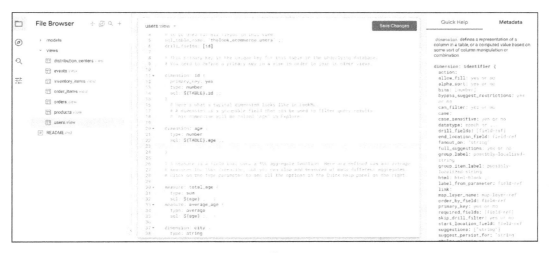

Figure 2.5 – The users view

Let's explore adding dimension parameters or creating new dimensions in our views.

How to do it...

Let's start with the following parameter: `drill_fields`. It specifies which fields will be "drilled" into when a user clicks on a cell for this field. For example, we want to give our Looker analysts the option to drill down by users' ages to check what the users' IDs for every age are. The steps for this are as follows:

1. Press Enter on your keyboard to start a new line after the `sql: ${TABLE}.age ;;` line and add `drill_fields: [id]` (*Figure 2.6*).

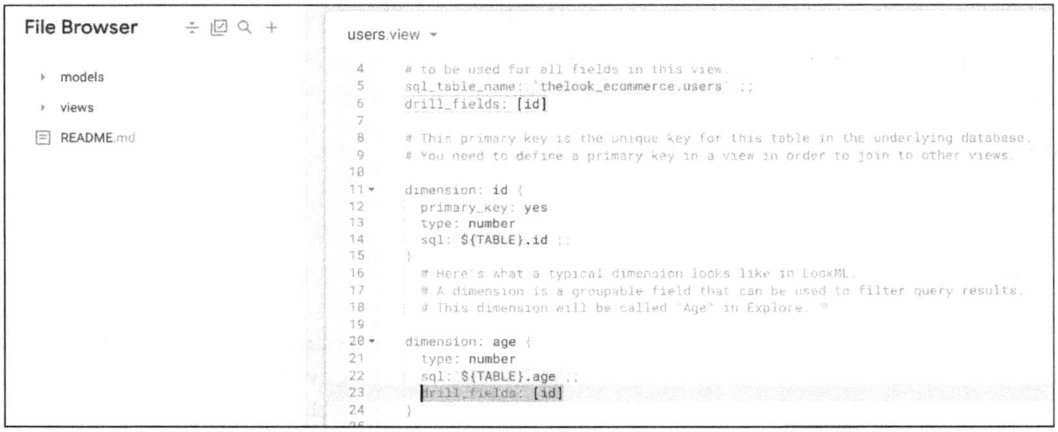

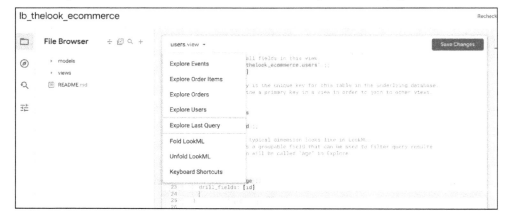

Figure 2.6 – Drill fields

2. Click on **Save Changes** above the editor on your right and once everything is saved, click on the drop-down list near `users.view` and choose **Explore Users** (*Figure 2.7*).

Figure 2.7 – Explores

3. In **Users** Explore, choose the `Age` and `Count` columns and press **Run**.

4. If you click on `18`, you will see the option to drill by the ID field (*Figure 2.8*); click on **by ID**.

Users Age ↑	⚙ Users Count
1	12
2	13
3	14
4	15
5	16
6	17
7	18
8	1 Drill into 18
9	2 by ID
10	2 Explore
11	2 Filter on "18"
12	2

Figure 2.8 – Drill by ID

5. Explore the user IDs of the users who are 18 years old.

6. Close the pop-up window with the users' IDs and go back to the LookML environment by clicking on **Go to LookML** in the bottom-left corner. If you don't see this option, you might need to activate **Development Mode**; click on it in the bottom-left corner of the hamburger menu.

In the `users.view`, Looker automatically added a set of field details that can be reused in different dimensions and measures, (*Figure 2.9*). This is another way of using the `drill_fields` parameter. Note that you can define your own sets as well.

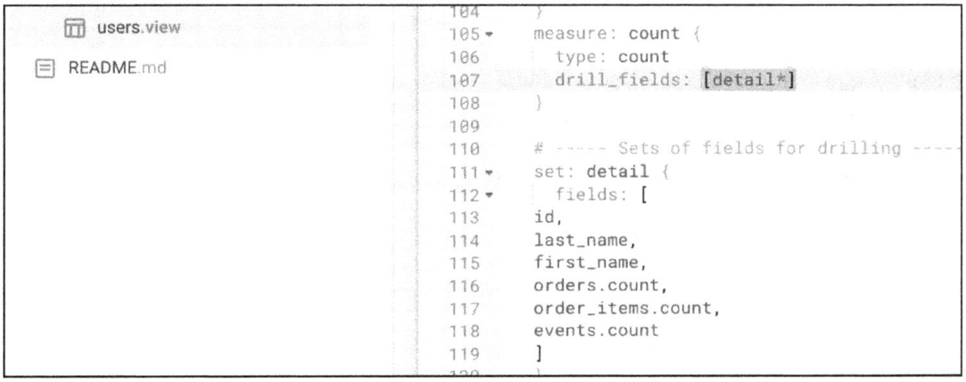

```
                                104     }
   ▥  users.view               105 ▾   measure: count {
                                106       type: count
   ☰  README.md                 107       drill_fields: [detail*]
                                108     }
                                109
                                110     # ----- Sets of fields for drilling ----
                                111 ▾   set: detail {
                                112 ▾     fields: [
                                113       id,
                                114       last_name,
                                115       first_name,
                                116       orders.count,
                                117       order_items.count,
                                118       events.count
                                119     ]
                                120     }
```

Figure 2.9 – Drill fields

Adding a new parameter: hidden

A second parameter we'll be adding in this chapter is hidden. It hides a field from the Explore if, for example, there is a field that is unnecessary for the analysis (note that granting access control should be the primary method for protecting sensitive data, not relying solely on hiding it). The steps to create and test this parameter are as follows:

1. In the users view, find the first_name and last_name dimensions and add a new line in these dimensions: hidden: yes; (*Figure 2.10*).

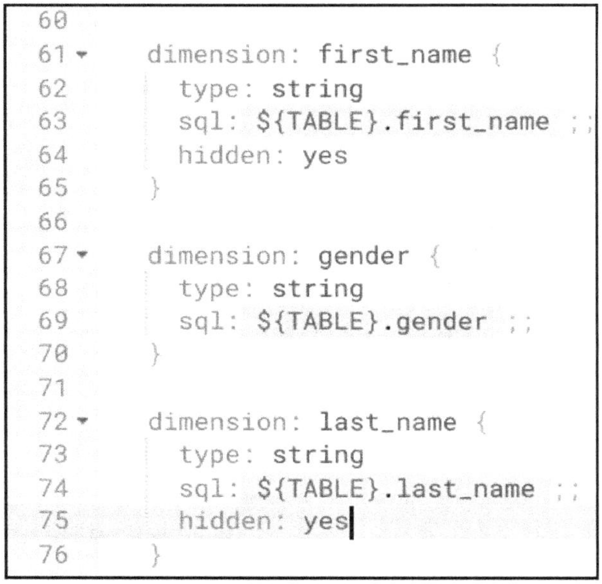

```
60
61 ▾    dimension: first_name {
62         type: string
63         sql: ${TABLE}.first_name ;;
64         hidden: yes
65      }
66
67 ▾    dimension: gender {
68         type: string
69         sql: ${TABLE}.gender ;;
70      }
71
72 ▾    dimension: last_name {
73         type: string
74         sql: ${TABLE}.last_name ;;
75         hidden: yes
76      }
```

Figure 2.10 – Hidden

2. Click on **Save Changes** and click on a drop-down list near user.view and go to **Explore Users** to check whether the first_name and last_name fields are invisible.

Creating a dimension based on the existing one

Now, let's create a completely new dimension based on our existing one:

1. Copy the following code and add it to your users.view file under any existing dimension:

```
dimension: full_name {
  type: string
  sql: ${first_name} || ' , ' || ${last_name};;
}
```

2. Click **Save Changes** and go check **Explore Users** as we did previously.

3. In the **Explore** environment, find the Full Name column, click on it, and then press **Run** to see the result.

Grouping users by age with a new dimension

What if we wanted to group our users by age group? Let's create a new dimension with the tier type for that:

1. Add the following code after any existing dimension in users.view:

    ```
    dimension: age_group {
       type: tier
       tiers: [18, 25, 35, 45, 55, 65, 75, 90]
       sql: ${age} ;;
       style: classic
    }
    ```

2. Click **Save Changes** and go to **Explore Users** in the drop-down list near users.view, above the editor window.

3. In **Explore Users**, choose the Age and Count column, then click **Run** (*Figure 2.11*). You will get a number of users per age group.

Figure 2.11 – Measure Count

4. In the dimension code, type specifies the value type of the field, and in this case, our type is tier. tier defines the numerical ranges used in a type: tier field. style defines the way that tiers appear in the Looker UI for a type: tier dimension (classic, interval, integer, or relational).

Creating "delivery time" dimension

Imagine you want to calculate how long it took to deliver an order in days. To do this, you can create a new dimension that will serve to show the delivery time. The steps to create and test this new dimension are as follows:

1. In your LookML project, open the `orders.view` in the code editor and add the following code after any dimension:

    ```
    dimension: delivery_time {
      type: number
      sql: DATE_DIFF(${delivered_date}, ${created_date}, day) ;;
    }
    ```

2. To understand whether our new dimension works as planned, go to **Explore Orders** (this time, we work with `order.view`) and choose the `delivery_time`, `delivery_date`, and `created_date` columns. Press **Run**.

3. You will see that our new dimension reuses our two existing dimensions, `created` and `delivery`, but the `date` type dimensions in Looker usually have some kind of subdimensions in the `timeframes` parameter (raw, time, date, week, month, quarter, or year), which is why our dimension reference transforms to `created_date` from `created` to specify the exact date and not week, month, quarter, and so on.

4. Don't forget that to go back to your LookML environment, you click on **Go to LookML** in the bottom-left corner in the Explore environment.

Creating a dimension based on the SQL query

Dimensions in Looker can be created using a complete SQL query inside the `SQL` parameter; as an example, let's look at the following dimension:

1. In the `orders.view`, add the following code after any dimension:

    ```
    dimension: reporting_period {
      sql:
      CASE
        WHEN EXTRACT(YEAR from ${created_raw}) =
          EXTRACT(YEAR from CURRENT_TIMESTAMP())
          AND ${created_raw} < CURRENT_TIMESTAMP()
        THEN 'This Year to Date'

        WHEN EXTRACT(YEAR from ${created_raw}) + 1 =
          EXTRACT(YEAR from CURRENT_TIMESTAMP())
          AND CAST(FORMAT_TIMESTAMP('%j',${created_raw})
          AS INT64) <= CAST(FORMAT_TIMESTAMP
    ```

```
            ('%j',CURRENT_TIMESTAMP()) AS INT64)
        THEN 'Last Year to Date'
        END;;
    }
```

2.   Click **Save Changes** and go to **Explore Orders**.

3.   In **Explore Orders**, choose `Created Date | Date` and `Reporting Period`, click **Run**, and analyze this result (*Figure 2.12*).

Figure 2.12 – Reporting Period

As you can see, the last dimension uses the SQL command CASE WHEN to define the reporting period depending on the order creation date and today's date.

How it works...

In Looker LookML, dimensions are fields that can be used to group, filter, and segment data. They can be any type of data, such as text, numbers, dates, and locations.

Dimensions are defined using the `dimension` parameter in LookML. This parameter specifies the name of the dimension and its type.

Once you have defined your dimensions in LookML, you can use them in Explores to create visualizations, which are the building blocks of Looker dashboards.

Explores allow you to specify the dimensions and measures that you want to include in your analysis.

Let's explore measures in the next section.

There's more...

To see how newly created and changed dimensions work in **Explore**, you can keep the **Explore** tab and the **LookML project** tab open in your browser and refresh the **Explore** page every time you make and save changes in the LookML view.

See also

- Explore different dimension types that you can use in Looker in this documentation section: https://cloud.google.com/looker/docs/reference/param-dimension-filter-parameter-types

Creating measures in views

Measures in Looker are aggregations of one or more dimensions (or unique attributes of the data) such as a count or average. They are used to calculate **key performance indicators** (**KPIs**) and help business users analyze data using different aggregated attributes. Three of the most common measure types are sum, average, and count. Measures represent the quantitative information in Looker.

By combining measures and dimensions, you can create visualizations and dashboards that help you understand both the quantitative and qualitative aspects of your business.

When you create your LookML project and choose **Generate Model** from **Database Schema**, Looker will automatically create Count measures for your tables (views). In Your LookML environment, go and check what are the measures that were created in your views. For example, the following measures in distribution_centers.view might not be relevant for your data exploration and might not make sense at all:

```
measure: total_latitude {
  type: sum
  sql: ${latitude};;
}

measure: average_latitude {
  type: average
  sql: ${latitude};;
}
```

> **Note:**
> Additional measure generation can occur if the 'Improved LookML Generation' feature is enabled in the **Admin** -> **General** -> **Labs** section.

Let's explore the useful measures created by Looker and create our own measures as well.

Getting ready

In this section, we will learn to modify our existing measures or create new ones. The number of parameters that can be added to the measures in Looker is quite large as well. If you click on the `orders.view` and click *Enter* after the SQL line (or any other line) in one of the measures, you will see on your right, in the **Quick Help** section, multiple parameters that can be added to the measure.

Let's work with the `orders.view`.

How to do it...

One of the measures created by Looker is the total number of items that calculates the sum of all the products ordered:

```
measure: total_num_of_item {
  type: sum
  sql: ${num_of_item} ;;
}
```

If we want to analyze the sum of items per month, we have everything we need for this:

1. In `orders.view`, click on the drop-down list ▼ above the code editor, as usual, to go to **Explore Orders**.

2. Choose the `Delivered Date|Month`, and `Total Num of Item` columns. You can add `Average Num of Item` as well.

3. Press **Run**. Explore the results (*Figure 2.13*).

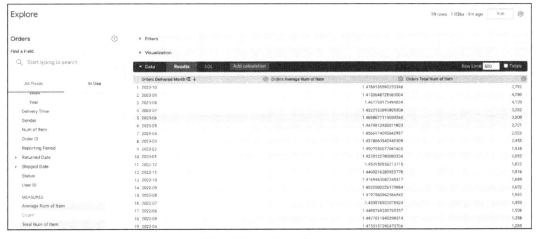

Figure 2.13 – Num of Items

You might see that the data format might be slightly improved – for example, for `Average Num of Item`, we don't necessarily need all these figures after a period. How can we change that?

Changing value format in measure

Let's go back to our LookML environment by clicking on **Go To LookML**. Make sure you are in `orders.view` by clicking on **Views** in the left panel, then click on `orders.view`. To modify the measure, do the following:

1. Find the `average_num_of_item` measure, and click *Enter* after the `type: sum` line, for example, to add a new parameter.

2. Add the `value_format: "0.0"` line.

3. Click **Save Changes**.

4. In `orders.view`, click on the drop-down list ▼ above the code editor, as usual, to go to **Explore Orders**.

5. Choose the `Delivered Date | Month`, and `Average Num of Item` columns.

6. You will see that the `Average Num of Item` format has changed.

Creating measure based on existing dimension

What measures might we need for further analysis? What KPIs might our colleagues need? Let's create new measures that Looker didn't create for us.

In the previous section, we created the `delivery_time` dimension:

```
dimension: delivery_time {
  type: number
  sql: DATE_DIFF(${delivered_date}, ${created_date}, day) ;;
}
```

If we want to have an average number of days spent on delivery per month to understand when we did better, we can create a measure for that:

1. After the `delivery_time` (the one that we created earlier in this chapter) dimension block in your `orders.view`, click *Enter* and add a new measure:

```
measure: average_days_to_process {
  type: average
  value_format_name: decimal_1
  sql: ${delivery_time} ;;
}
```

2. As usual, click **Save Changes**.

3. In `orders.view`, click on the drop-down list ▼ above the code editor, as usual, to go to **Explore Orders**.

4. Choose the `Delivered Date|Month`, and `Average Days to Process` columns.

5. Press **Run**. What are the best and the worst months in terms of average delivery time?

Creating Gross Margin measure

Let's try something more complicated. We will create a `total_gross_margin_percentage` measure, which will be based on the newly created dimension and measure. Total gross margin percentage is a financial metric that measures the profitability of a business by calculating the percentage of revenue that remains after the **cost of goods sold** (**COGS**) has been subtracted. The steps to do this are the following:

1. Open `orders_items.view` in your LookML environment. Add the following dimension after any of the existing dimension blocks. Pay attention to the fact that this dimension uses a dimension from another view, `inventory_items.cost`; if your views are not joined in the model file, this won't work (but it's likely that Looker did the joins for you):

    ```
    dimension: gross_margin {
      type: number
      value_format_name: usd
      sql: ${sale_price} - ${inventory_items.cost} ;;
    }
    ```

2. Add a measure to calculate a total gross margin:

    ```
    measure: total_gross_margin {
      type: sum
      value_format_name: usd
      sql: ${gross_margin} ;;
      drill_fields: [detail*]
    }
    ```

3. Add a new measure that will be based on the existing `total_gross_margin` and `total_sales_price` measures:

    ```
    measure: total_gross_margin_percentage {
      type: number
      value_format_name: percent_2
      sql: 1.0 * ${total_gross_margin}/
           nullif(${total_sale_price},0) ;;
    }
    ```

4. As usual, click **Save Changes**.

5. In `order_items.view`, click on the drop-down list ▼ above the code editor as usual to go to Explore Order Items.

6. Choose columns in the Order Items group of columns: `Delivery Date | Month`, `Total Gross Margin`, `Total Gross Margin Percentage`, and `Total Sales Price` (*Figure 2.14*).

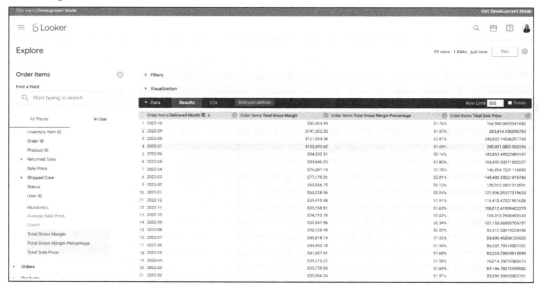

Figure 2.14 – Total Gross Margin

Are you happy with the result? What would you change or improve?

How it works...

Measures in Looker are quantitative values calculated by performing aggregations on data from one or more dimensions, other measures, or through standalone calculations. They are used to calculate KPIs and other metrics that help business users analyze data and make better decisions.

Measures can be created using a variety of SQL aggregate functions, such as `sum`, `average`, `min`, `max`, and `count_distinct`. They can also be combined to create more complex calculations (note that most SQL dialects are unable to double aggregate or nest aggregations). For example, you could create a measure that calculates the year-over-year growth of sales.

Measures are used in Looker to create visualizations, such as charts and tables. They can also be used to filter data and create calculated fields.

There's more...

To see how newly created and changed measures work in the **Explore** tab, you can keep the **Explore** tab and the **LookML project** tab open in your browser and refresh the **Explore** page every time you make and save changes in the LookML view.

See also

- Explore different measure types that you can use in Looker in this documentation section: `https://cloud.google.com/looker/docs/reference/param-measure-types`

Describing data in LookML views

Everything you do in LookML is aimed at making your data clean, complete, well organized, and ready to be used. There are numerous ways to describe and organize your data in LookML. In this section, we will go through some of the parameters to do so.

Getting ready

Let's continue working in `order_items.view`. Make sure you have it open in your LookML environment. When working with the *How to do it...* section, try all the provided parameters in your environment. Don't forget to click **Save Changes** to see how it all looks in the **Explore** tab.

How to do it...

The different parameters you can use to organize your dimensions and measures in views (*Figure 2.15*) and make it clear and accessible are the following:

- **Comments**: The comments in LookML start with #. The automatic comments are added by Looker when the views and model were created in your project in **Database Schema**. Review the comments and make some changes. Add your comment before the dimensions and measures you created.

- **Hidden**: The `hidden:yes` parameter is something that we explored already. It is used to hide some fields from the Explores. It can be used when the dimension or measure is not necessary to be displayed (because, for example, it only exists to be used in the newly created dimension). Note that this parameter is not secure for sensitive information.

- **Description**: The `description: ""` parameter is used to describe your dimension or measure, to explain it to the analysts and all the other users who will work with the Explores.

- **Label:** The `label` parameter lets you change how a field name will appear in the field picker. If you don't specify a label, the field name will be used instead. (You can use `group_item_label` in dimensions and measures that contain `group_label`.)

- **Group label:** Use `group_label` to group related fields together in the field picker.

- **Tags:** The `tags` parameter lets you specify a list of text strings that can be used to add additional information about a field. This information can be read by machines and accessed via the API.

- **Suggestable:** The `suggestable` parameter lets you turn off suggestions for string dimensions and filters. By default, suggestions are turned on. If you set suggestable to no, suggestions will be turned off. Check the `suggest_dimension` parameter as well. Use `suggest_dimension` to make Looker query an alternative dimension for the suggestion values.

- **Value format:** You can use `value_format` at the field level to apply formatting to a specific dimension or measure, or at the model level to create a reusable custom format that can be applied to multiple fields.

- **Value format name:** Use the `value_format_name` parameter to format data values using built-in or custom Looker formats.

Figure 2.15 – Data description

The view itself can contain multiple organization/description parameters, such as the following:

- **Fields hidden by default**: Set `fields_hidden_by_default:` to `yes` to hide all fields in the view by default. This value can be overridden by applying `hidden: no` to a given field.

- **Label**: The name of the view that will appear in the Explore UI when this view is joined in.

- **View label**: `view_label` defines how a group of fields from a joined view will be labeled in the field picker.

- **Set**: Sets are useful for grouping fields that need to be used together in other parameters, such as fields (for joins) and `drill_fields` (for fields). To define a set, use the `set` parameter. You can include any number of dimensions, measures, or filter fields from the current view in a set, including the individual dimensions generated by a dimension group (*Figure 2.16*).

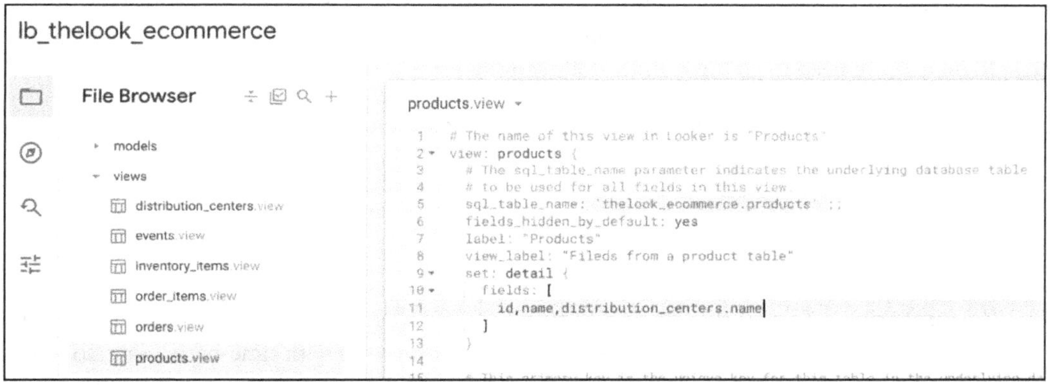

Figure 2.16 – View parameters

Working with filters in LookML views

There are two main types of filters in LookML:

- **Explore-level filters**: These let you restrict the data that you are viewing to rows of interest. Any field in your Looker instance can become a filter.

- **Field-level filters**: These filters are applied to a specific field in the view and can be used to restrict the data that is available for that field in all Explores that use the field.

In this section, we will concentrate on the filters used in the LookML views.

Getting ready

For the examples in this section, we will work with `inventory_items.view` in the LookML project environment.

How to do it...

The different filter-related parameters that can be used in the views are the following:

- **Can filter**: The `can_filter` parameter lets you prohibit a dimension or measure from being used as a filter.

- **Skip drill filter**: If `skip_drill_filter` is yes, this dimension will not be included in drill filters.

- **Filters**: `filters` is an optional list of filter expressions that are applied to a measure calculation, and works only with the following measure types that perform aggregation: `count`, `count_distinct`, `sum`, and `average`.

So, how do you use `filters`? For example, while working on `inventory_items.view`, we want to add a measure that follows the percentage of products sold (by brand, category, or product itself). To do this, we need to go through the following steps:

1. Create a dimension that tracks whether the item is sold or not:

```
dimension: is_sold {
  type: yesno
  sql: ${sold_raw} is not null ;;
}
```

The dimension sold uses `dimension_group : sold`. The dimension group is a set of related dimensions. Currently, dimension groups are only used with time-based data, so they should have `type: time` or `type: duration`. So, here we take the Sold dimension group with the date "raw".

2. Now, let's create the measure that counts the items that are sold:

```
measure: sold_count {
  type: count
  filters: {
    field: is_sold
    value: "Yes"
  }
}
```

That's where we use our `filters` parameter.

3. Our final measure, the one that responds to our initial question and is based on the previous dimension and measure created, looks like this:

```
measure: sold_percent {
  type: number
  value_format_name: percent_2
```

```
sql: 1.0 * ${sold_count}/(CASE WHEN ${count} = 0 THEN NULL
    ELSE ${count} END) ;;
}
```

4. Click **Save Changes** and go to **Explore Inventory Items** to see whether your new measure works.

5. Choose the `Product Brand`, `Sold Percent`, `Sold Count`, and `Count` columns. Press **Run**. (In *Figure 2.17*, we sort by the `Count` column.)

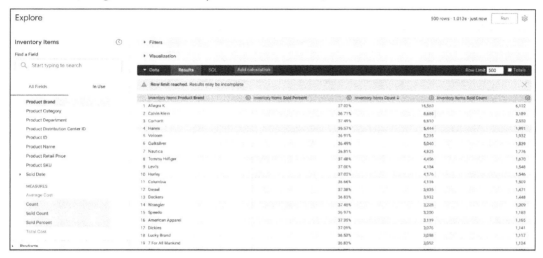

Figure 2.17 – Products sold

Filters can contain multiple dimensions to filter on:

```
view: view_name {
  measure: field_name {
  filters: [dimension_name: "filter expression",
          dimension_name: "filter expression", ... ]
  }
}
```

Joining tables in models

In this section, we will work on our model file. Every LookML project can contain multiple model files if needed. Model files define Explores and their relationships to other views. Models can be placed in the **Models** section of the Looker IDE. The model's name is taken from the filename and must be unique across your instance.

Getting ready

In this section, we will work on our unique `lb_thelook_ecommerce.model` model file.

In your LookML project in the left panel, click on models and then click on `lb_thelook_ecommerce.model`. Our existing model contains multiple parameters and Explores. Explores can be declared (created) based on one view or multiple views joined.

How to do it...

1. To create an Explore based on one view (for example, `distrubution_centers.view`), the syntax is simple:

   ```
   explore: distribution_centers {}
   ```

2. In the preceding case, the Explore name equals the base view name. In a Looker Explore, the base view is the initial data source for the Explore. It typically represents either a database table or a LookML-defined derived table

3. If you want to name your Explore differently, add a `label` parameter:

   ```
   explore: distribution_centers {
     label: "DC"
   }
   ```

Creating Explore based on multiple views

Let's learn how to create the Explores based on two or more joined views:

1. The following parameters are necessary to perform joins:

   - `primary_key`: Make sure that you have the `primary_key` parameter in the views that will be joined.

   - `join`: The main parameter to join views. The `join` parameter only takes a view name, not the table name associated with that view. Join usually contains the following parameters:

     - `type`: The `type` parameter can be cross, `left_outer` (default if not specified), `full_outer`, inner.

     - `sql_on`: The `sql_on` parameter establishes a join relationship between a view and its Explore, based on a SQL ON clause that you provide. For LookML, the order of conditions in `sql_on` does not matter. Conditional joins can be used as well.

     - `relationship`: This parameter lets you describe the join relationship between joined views. It's important to properly define the type of relationship for Looker to calculate accurate measures.

2. As an example, let's take a look at the LookML code for an Explore built from two views automatically generated by Looker. This code can be found in your model file:

```
explore: products {
  join: distribution_centers {
    type: left_outer
    sql_on: ${products.distribution_center_id} =
            ${distribution_centers.id} ;;
    relationship: many_to_one
  }
}
```

3. This Explore based on two views will be automatically named after the first view used. If you want to name it differently, use the label parameter. Click on **Save Changes** after making the modifications (*Figure 2.18*).

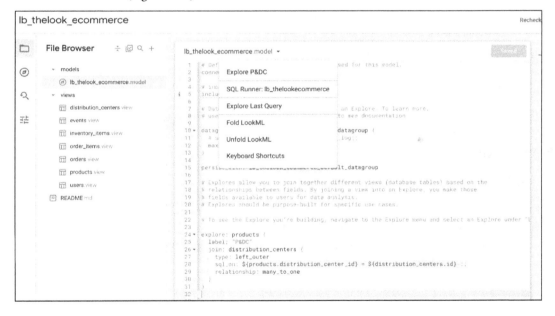

Figure 2.18 – Joins

More parameters can be used in joins; you'll find these parameters in the link at the end of this section.

See also

- Join parameters: `https://cloud.google.com/looker/docs/reference/param-join`

Adding advanced model parameters

In the model file created in your LookML project, there are some standard parameters added, such as the following:

- `connection`: This parameter defines the database/data warehouse connection to be used for this model.

- `include`: This defines what view files can be used in this model to build the Explores. In our case, we include all the views.

- `datagroup`: This assigns a caching policy for Explores. Datagroup can also be used to regenerate PDTs.

- `persist_with`: To use the `datagroup` caching policy as the default for Explores in a model, you can use the `persist_with` parameter at the model level, and specify the `datagroup` name.

In this section, we'll review some advanced Model parameters and what they are used for.

How to do it...

Let's add a few advanced Model parameters to our model:

1. `label`: The `label` parameter changes the way that this model will appear in the **Explore** menu. Unless specified, the label defaults to the name of the model with underscores replaced with spaces and each word capitalized. Let's add a meaningful name to our model after the `connection` line:

   ```
   label: "Our Company Ecommerce Data Model"
   ```

2. `week_start_day`: We want to define Monday as the first day of the week for all our Explores, so we want to specify that on the Model level. For this, let's add the following line:

   ```
   week_start_day: monday
   ```

3. `named_value_format`: The `named_value_format` parameter lets you create and save a custom format that can be applied to multiple dimensions and measures. Let's add the following `named_value_format` to our model:

   ```
   named_value_format: percent_with_no_decimals {
     value_format: "0\%"
   }
   ```

4. Now, we can reuse this custom format in our measures using the `value_format_name` parameter, for example, in our `sold_percent` measure in `inventory_items.view`:

```
measure: sold_percent {
  type: number
  value_format_name: percent_with_no_decimals
  sql: 1.0 * ${sold_count}/(CASE WHEN ${count} = 0 THEN NULL
    ELSE ${count} END) ;;
}
```

Other advanced model parameters include `persist_for`, `access_grant`, `test`, `case_sensitive`, `fiscal_month_offset`, `map_layer`, and `map_layer_name`. We'll explore map parameters later in this chapter.

There's more...

Derived tables in Looker are temporary or persistent tables that are created from the results of a query. They can be used to simplify complex queries, improve performance, or create new datasets that are not available in your underlying database.

There are two types of derived tables in Looker:

- **Native-derived tables** are defined with a LookML-based query
- **SQL-based derived tables** are defined with an SQL query

Derived tables can be temporary or persistent. **Persistent derived tables** (PDTs) are created using LookML and are stored in your underlying database. They are typically used to improve performance or to create new datasets that are frequently used.

To create a derived table in Looker, you use the `derived_table` parameter in the view file. The `derived_table` parameter specifies the query that will be used to create the table.

It can be created with the `explore_source` (with a view or views as a source) or `SQL` (with an SQL query as a source) parameter.

Derived tables can be used to create Explores in the Model just like regular views.

To make a derived table persistent in Looker, add Looker-managed persistence parameters such as `datagroup_trigger`, `sql_trigger_value`, `interval_trigger`, or `persist_for` to the `derived_table` definition.

You will see an example of a derived table in the *Working with geodata in LookML* section.

See also

- Read more about the Model parameters here: `https://cloud.google.com/looker/docs/reference/param-model`

- Documentation about derived tables: `https://cloud.google.com/looker/docs/reference/param-view-derived-table`

Working with LookML files

Your LookML project can contain multiple different files. We already worked with view and model files, and we could see what the folders are for (models and views folders). You can create a new folder or file by pressing + (*Figure 2.19*).

Figure 2.19 – LookML files

Let's add some more elements to enrich our LookML project.

Getting ready

Make sure you are in your LookML project environment with **Development Mode** activated (see the blue bar at the top of your Looker web page).

How to do it...

Let's add some information about our LookML project:

1. Click on the README.md file – in there, you will see some explanations about Looker; keep it as it is.

2. Let's add another document file to add some information about our e-commerce project – click the + sign near **File Browser** and click on **Create Document**.

3. Name the document AboutThisProject and click **Create**.

4. Click **Edit** and add the following lines:

   This is e-commerce data about worldwide orders from a fictitious shop.

5. Add any other information that you find useful.

6. Click **Save Changes**.

7. Now, users will have more information about our LookML project once they are in it.

Adding new tables from your dataset

If you added a new table to your dataset in BigQuery, you might want to add it to your LookML project:

1. Click on the + sign near **File Browser**.

2. Click on **Create View from Table**.

3. Choose the new table (if you had added one) or any other table if you want to create a different view with the same table.

4. Click **Create View**. The **Create Model** and **Create View** options let you create new models and views from scratch.

Create Dashboard gives you the possibility to have your dashboard in a code – that might be useful, for example, for version control of your dashboards in a git environment.

Localization in LookML project

Create Locale Strings Files will contain key-value pairs to define how the labels and descriptions in your model are displayed for each locale. For example, if we have Spanish-speaking users, we can create the following for them:

1. Click on the + sign near **File Browser**.

2. Choose **Create Locale Strings Files**.

3. Name it es_ES.strings.json and click **Create**.

4. Delete all the text that is automatically added to the created file. Add the following elements to this file:

```
{
    "name": "Nombre",
    "id": "Identificador",
    "order": "Orden",
    "country": "País",
    "product": "Producto",
}
```

5. Click **Save Changes**.

Creating Project Manifest

1. Now, to enable localization for your project, you need to add the `localization_settings` parameter to your project's manifest file.

2. To set a localization for a user, you need to modify the **Locale User Attribute** in **Admin | Users | User Attributes**. We'll explore **User Attributes** later in this book.

    Create Project Manifest lets you create a text file that contains configuration settings for your Looker project. The project manifest file can be used to specify other projects to import into the current project, specify model localization settings, define LookML constants, and add extensions and custom visualizations to your project. Let's create a manifest file:

3. Click on the **+** sign near **File Browser**.

4. Click on **Create Project Manifest** (it is unique for every project; you won't be able to create it if you already have one).

5. Delete everything in the file and add the following:

```
localization_settings: {
    default_locale: en
    localization_level: permissive
}
```

6. Click **Save Changes**.

7. The default locale is used to determine valid localized keys and their default values when the localization level is set to `permissive`. Localization level controls how strict Looker is about missing localization translations. At the strict level, Looker will return an error for any missing translation or any locale definition that does not implement all of the keys in the default locale definition. At the permissive level, Looker will show an information message instead of an error

8. You can add additional files to your LookML project such as the TopoJSON or GeoJSON files to provide geographical data to be used in `map_layer`. For this, you just need to have the file on your local computer and then drag and drop it into the LookML project (see *Figure 2.20;* image from official documentation).

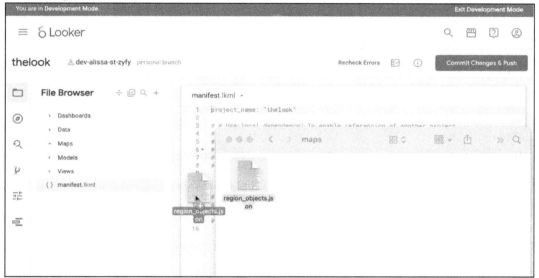

Figure 2.20 – Uploading a file (image from official documentation)

We'll use this file-uploading option in the next section.

See also

- Types of files in LookML documentation: `https://cloud.google.com/looker/docs/lookml-project-files`

Working with geodata in LookML

Geodata in your tables gives you the possibility to create map chart visualizations. In this section, we will have the opportunity to use the things we previously learned in combination with some new elements related to geodata.

Getting ready

You will need to download the following file to your computer, then drag and drop this file in your LookML environment (as shown in the previous section): communes.topojson - `https://github.com/PacktPublishing/Business-Intelligence-with-Looker-Cookbook/blob/main/communes.topojson`. This file contains the coordinates of the French communes – cities, towns, villages – local administrative units.

To visualize the geodata in a map chart, you need to include at least one of the following fields in your query: a dimension based on latitude and longitude data, a dimension with a map layer assigned to it, or a ZIP code dimension.

> **Note**
> According to the documentation, a ZIP code dimension automatically has a US ZIP code map layer assigned to it. This is defined by a LookML developer as a dimension of type: zipcode. ZIP code regions are based on the US **ZIP Code Tabulation Areas (ZCTAs)**. However, there may not be a one-to-one correspondence between ZIP codes and the ZCTAs used for map visualizations. It is possible that not all points will be visualized on the map.

How to do it...

Now that we have our file with French administrative units prepared, we will use it to show different data points per city (for example, the number of customers per city) on the map. To do this, you need to follow these steps:

1. First of all, let's create a new view based on a derived table to have only France in this view:

    I.   Click on **+** near **File Browser**.

    II.   Click on **Create View** and name it users_france.

    III. Delete all the elements automatically added in the view and add the following code:

    ```
    view: users_france {
      derived_table: {
        sql:
        SELECT *
        FROM users
        WHERE country = "France"
        ;;
      }
    }
    ```

2. Copy all the dimensions and measures from users.view and paste them into users_
    france.view, after the code block we have already added in users_france.view. It
    will look something like the following figure:

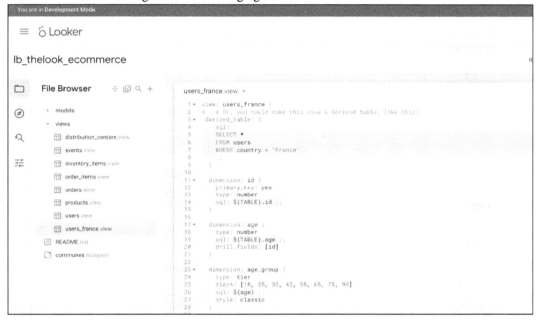

Figure 2.21 – View derived table

3. Now, let's open our Model file and do the following:

4. First, create the Explore based on your new users_france view:

```
explore: users_france {
```

-   Then, before or after this code (the order is not important), add the following parameter:

```
map_layer: communes {
   file: "/communes.topojson"
   format: topojson
}
```

5. Click **Save Changes**.

Working with the map layer

map_layer defines a mapping from a data value to a geographic region as well as a data source for the shape of the geographic region.

1. Open users_france.view and find the dimension city, add the following line in this dimension map_layer_name: communes. Your City dimension will look like this:

    ```
    dimension: city {
       type: string
       sql: ${TABLE}.city ;;
       map_layer_name: communes
    }
    ```

2. Click **Save Changes**.

3. In the drop-down menu near users_france.view above the code editor, click on ▼ and choose **Explore Users France**.

4. In **Explore Users France**, choose the City (place where our users live) and Count (how many users we have in our database) columns to get the number of customers per city.

5. Press **Run** and then **Sort by Count** (click on the Count column in the Results table) to have the cities with the biggest number of users at the top.

6. Open the visualization section above Results and choose **Google Maps** visualization (see *Figure 2.22*).

Figure 2.22 – Maps

The cities wouldn't be mapped without `map_layer` being added to Model and then reused in the view on the dimension level.

Working with latitude and longitude dimensions

In one of our views, you might have seen latitude and longitude dimensions. How do we work with those? Let's follow these steps:

1. Open `distribution_centers.view`.

2. Add the following dimension:

    ```
    dimension: dc_location {
      type: location
      sql_latitude: ${TABLE}.latitude ;;
      sql_longitude: ${TABLE}.longitude ;;
    }
    ```

3. Click **Save Changes**.

4. This dimension combines your latitude and longitude dimensions in order to create a geodata dimension with the `type: location` parameter. You might want to add the `hidden: yes` parameter to `dimension: longitude` and `dimension: latitude` – it doesn't make sense to show them in the Explores.

5. Use the `type: location` dimension to create geographic coordinates for Map and Static Map (Points) visualizations, or to use in `type: distance` calculations. For Static Map (Regions) visualizations, use a state or country field.

6. In LookML project open the `users.view` file that contains latitude and longitude dimensions as well, and add the same dimension:

    ```
    dimension: users_location {
      type: location
      sql_latitude: ${TABLE}.latitude ;;
      sql_longitude: ${TABLE}.longitude ;;
    }
    ```

7. Now, let's add the distance calculation to our `users.view` so we will be able to calculate and visualize how far away our users are from our distribution centers:

    ```
    dimension: distance_to_DCs {
      type: distance
      start_location_field: distribution_centers.dc_location
      end_location_field: users_location
      units: kilometers
    }
    ```

8. You might want to check whether your **View Users** is joined with **View Distribution Center** before going to **Explore**. Go to model and make sure they are connected. The **Explore** that connects multiple tables in our model starts with the following:

```
explore: order_items {
    join: users {...
```

9. Let's add the `label: "All Ecommerce Tables Joined"` line to make the name of our Explore more meaningful.

10. Click **Save Changes**.

11. In the drop-down menu near `lb_thelook_ecommerce.model` above the code editor, click on ▼ and choose **Explore All Ecommerce Tables Joined**.

12. Choose the `Users Location`, `DC Location`, and `Distance to DC` columns. Press **Run**.

13. In the Filters section, add Filters Country = "France" and City="Marseille".

14. In the Visualization section, choose **Google Maps**, then click on **Edit** in the right corner of the Visualization block, then scroll to find the **Connect with Areas** option.

15. It looks like our Marseille customers get their orders from the Distribution Center all over the US (*Figure 2.23*). This might open the discussion about delivery optimization.

Figure 2.23 – Distance

Now, let's go to the last section of this chapter to find out how to reuse elements in LookML.

Reusing the LookML code

There are multiple ways to reuse the elements in LookML, such as the following:

- `include`
- `extends`
- `${}`
- Refinements
- Looker Blocks

We've already used $ quite a lot to reference the existing dimensions and measures.

We have also used the `include` parameter, which specifies the LookML files that will be available to a model, a view, and an Explore. If you want to use or reference a LookML file within another file, you must add it with the `include` parameter.

Let's review some other techniques you can use to reuse elements in Looker.

Getting ready

Make sure you are in your LookML environment, and **Development Mode** is activated.

How to do it...

The `extends` parameters can be used both for views and Explores. For example, you can use the `extends` parameter in views to reuse the content and settings of another view, with the ability to override any settings that you want.

We can learn how to do that by following these steps:

1. Click on + near **File Browser**, click on **Create View**, and name it `users_statistics`.
2. In the newly created view, delete all the automatically added text and add the following code:

```
include: "users.view"
view: users_statistics {
  extends: [users]

  measure: count_percent_of_total {
    label: "Count (Percent of Total)"
    type: percent_of_total
    sql: ${count} ;;
    drill_fields: [detail*]
  }
```

```
measure: average_age {
  type: average
  value_format_name: decimal_2
  sql: ${age} ;;
  drill_fields: [detail*]
}
```

The extends: [users] line means that in this new view, we take everything from the users.view to make the users.view visible in this new view, we used the parameter include: "users.view"

After the extends block, we added new measures. It means that our new Users Statistics view will contain all the columns from Users table + newly created measures.

3. Click **Save Changes** in the view. Make sure your view is in the views folder; if not, drag and drop it.

4. In the model, make sure to declare a new Explore based on the new view:

```
explore: users_statistics {}
```

5. Click **Save Changes** and go to **Explore Users Statistics** to analyze extends for a view. The extends can be used for scenarios where you want to have multiple versions of the view or Explore. If you want to simply modify a view or an Explore without editing the LookML file that contains it, you may want to use a refinement instead:

```
include: "/views/distribution_centers.view.lkml"

view: +distribution_centers {
  dimension: latitude {
    hidden: yes
  }
}
```

Looker Blocks, another functionality for reusing things and simplifying your work in Looker, are pre-built data models that you can use to quickly and easily analyze common data patterns. Choose from a variety of blocks in the Looker Marketplace, and then customize them to your exact needs. We will talk more about Looker Marketplace later in this book.

3
Working with Data in Explores

An Explore in Looker is a user-friendly interface that allows us to build queries against a data model without needing to write direct SQL code. Explore is the environment where users can build their visualizations based on one or multiple columns from one or multiple views (tables), applying custom filters, custom calculations, pivots, and so on if necessary. Explores are created in the model files in LookML and based on one or multiple views. Therefore, to create an Explore, you first need to define a view (or multiple views) using the `view` parameter. When created in a model file, an Explore can have additional configuration parameters, such as Description, Label, and Filters:

```
explore: users {
  # additional explore parameters go here
}
```

As you may remember, Looker licenses classify users into three types – Developer (Admin), Standard (Creator), Viewer. Only the first two can have access to the Explore environment. However, user management can be very granular in Looker, so in some cases, a Developer user won't have access to Explores, and Standard users (Creators) might not have access to certain Explores.

Explores in Looker are the starting point for data exploration. When you create a Look or dashboard tile in Looker, you select an Explore as the data source.

Explores are a powerful tool for data exploration and analysis. They allow you to easily and quickly ask questions about your data and get the answers you need.

Here are some of the advantages of Looker Explores:

- Explores are designed to be easy to use, even if you are not a SQL expert. You can simply select the fields you want to analyze, and Looker will generate the SQL query for you (based on the "instructions" provided in the LookML project).

- Explores are very powerful and can be used to perform complex data analysis. You can join multiple views, create custom calculations, and filter and group your data in a variety of ways.

- Explores are flexible and can be used to create a wide variety of data visualizations, including tables, charts, and maps.

In the previous chapters, we briefly used Explores to visualize our data, so you might be already familiar with the interface.

In this chapter, we will see how you can prepare your Explores in the model file using different parameters, and then we will use the Explore environment and its advanced parameters to build the visualization and share it and/or add it to the dashboard.

In this chapter, we're going to cover the following main recipes:

- Explore parameters in the model
- Advanced filtering in Explores
- Custom fields
- Pivoting and table manipulations in Explores
- Editing visualizations
- Merging data from multiple Explores

Technical requirements

There are no specific requirements or preparation steps for this chapter, so we will continue working with our **thelook_ecommerce** dataset (https://console.cloud.google.com/marketplace/product/bigquery-public-data/thelook-ecommerce), switching regularly between LookML and Explore environments inside Looker. We won't be working inside BigQuery (which is the data warehouse used in this book), as we assume our dataset is already connected to Looker and ready to be used in it. However, you can keep the BigQuery tab (*Figure 3.1*) open to preview the tables and get familiarized with the data you'll be exploring in Looker.

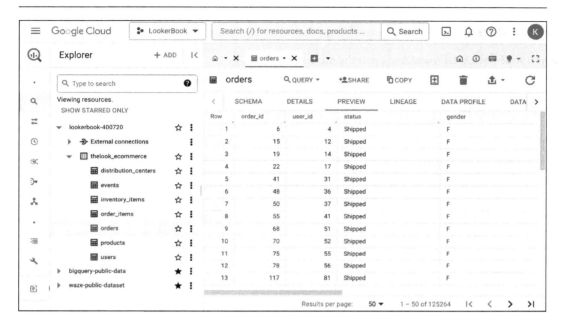

Figure 3.1—A BigQuery table preview

Open one tab with the LookML project environment and another tab with the BigQuery environment, and then we'll start exploring the data.

Exploring parameters in the model

As with all the elements in LookML, Explores in the model files have their own parameters to describe, filter, join data, define cache rules, and so on. Some of them are quite similar to other elements' parameters and are used to describe and organize the data – `tags`, `description`, `group_label`, `hidden`, `label`, `view_label`, `view_name`, `from`, and `fields`. The from parameter in an Explore specifies the view that provides the fields for it (explore: explore_name {from: view_name}). If it is omitted, Looker will assume that the underlying view has the same name as the Explore. The `fields` parameter lets you control which fields from an Explore are visible in the Explore user interface.

There are some parameters in Explores that help you to reuse existing elements, such as `extends` (to reuse and complete the existing Explore) and `persist_with` (to reuse the existing datagroup caching policy).

In this section, we will explore the most commonly utilized options to apply default filters to an Explore (the first two of the following cannot be changed by the Explore user) – `sql_always_where`, `sql_always_having`, `always_filter`, `conditionally_filter`, and `access_filter`.

Getting ready

Go to your LookML project and open the model file. We'll work in the model file on our Explores to set up some predefined filters that won't be visible to Standard (Creator) users.

How to do it...

Let's find the existing **Explore Orders**, based on the two joined tables, Orders and Users. This Explore is automatically named after the first View mentioned, **Orders**.

1. Copy this Explore, and paste it after your Orders block. You might encounter an error because the Explore name should be unique. You can rename your Explore orders_and_users and specify the view_name parameter that indicates the view (the first view in this case) on which an Explore will be based (*Figure 3.2*).

Figure 3.2 – Explore orders_and_users in the model

2. If you know what the WHERE and HAVING commands do in SQL, it is easy to understand the difference between sql_always_where and sql_always_having parameters. Both filter the Explore before it is shown to Standard users, with one difference:

- WHERE: To filter rows based on individual row values - on dimensions - before any grouping or aggregation: `sql_always_where: ${created_date} >= '2024-01-01' ;;`

- HAVING: To filter rows based on measures - on aggregated values: `sql_always_having: ${count} >= 100 ;;`

Let's say we want to limit our Users' data exploration to the orders placed after the year 2021. Why this might be the case? Let's say we changed our business model, website, and everything else in 2021, and comparing present data with the data gathered before these changes simply doesn't make sense. So, we want to make sure that our users never compare incomparable and never use the *before 2021* results for their analysis and dashboards.

3. Add the `sql_always_where` line to your **Orders and Users** Explore in the model:

```
explore: orders_and_users {
  view_name: orders
  sql_always_where: ${orders.created_year}>2021 ;;
  join: users {
    type: left_outer
    sql_on: ${orders.user_id} = ${users.id} ;;
    relationship: many_to_one
  }
}
```

4. To verify the results, save the changes, and then go to the **Orders and Users** Explore by clicking on it in the drop-down list near your model name, `lb_thelook_ecommerce.model`.

5. In the Explore environment, choose the `Created Date | Year` columns and then the column Count – note that the year 2021 and the years before (if they exist in our table) won't appear (*Figure 3.3*).

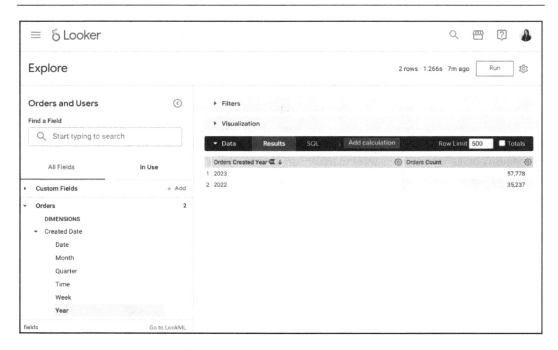

Figure 3.3 – Explore Orders_and_Users

6. Click **Go to LookML** in the bottom-left corner; this will open a new tab. As we'll continue working on the **Orders and Users** Explore, you can keep the Explore environment and the LookML model tabs open. Whenever you make a change to the Explore code in the LookML model, you can refresh the open tab with the Explore, and it will take all the changes into account.

7. Let's imagine that our Orders and Users table will serve only for the analysis of returning users who made more than three orders. In the LookML model file in our orders_and_users Explore, add the following code:

```
explore: orders_and_users {
  view_name: orders
  sql_always_where: ${orders.created_year}>2021 ;;
  sql_always_having: ${orders.count}>3  ;;
  join: users {
    type: left_outer
    sql_on: ${orders.user_id} = ${users.id} ;;
    relationship: many_to_one
  }
}
```

8. Go to your **Explore** tab and refresh it; then, choose the `User ID` and `Count` columns (`orders.count`) and click **Run**.

9. The **Results** section will show the users and the order quantity per user, which must be more than three. You can try to modify your filter to make it more than 1, more than 2, more than 3, and so on. Check the results that you get. Note: This filter behavior depends on the specific Looker query you run. The results may vary based on the data and filters applied.

10. Go back to the LookML project, open your model file, and in the `orders_and_users` Explore, add the following filter (*Figure 3.4*):

```
always_filter: {
  filters: [
    users.country: "United States"
  ]
}
```

    `always_filter` means that the Explore will always be filtered – in this case, by country, and the default value is `United States`. This default value can be changed by Explore users to another country, but the filter itself cannot be deleted. The filter is visible and appears above the visualization in the **Filters** section.

11. `conditionally_filter` means that you add a default filter that can be removed if at least one of the specified alternative filter fields is selected. It is used to prevent users from accidentally creating very large queries. For example, let's create a filter that will take the data for the last month only unless the specific user is analyzed (*Figure 3.4*):

```
conditionally_filter: {
  filters: [orders.created_month: "1 month"]
  unless: [users.id]
}
```

    Note: if you have No Results try 2, 3, or more months, data is not constantly updated.

12. `access_filter` lets you apply user-specific data restrictions; we will talk about it later in the book.

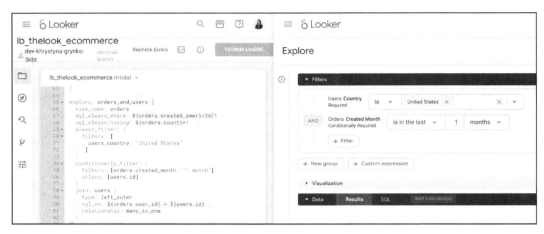

Figure 3.4 – Filters (the Explore and LookML tabs)

Empower business users to explore data and answer their own questions with well-crafted, intuitive Explores by customizing these Explores with parameters, revealing hidden insights and inspiring confidence in the data.

See also

- Read more about Explore parameters here: https://cloud.google.com/looker/docs/reference/param-explore.

Advanced filtering in Explores

Now, we'll work in our Explore environment only. Let's continue with the Explore we used in the previous section called **Orders and Users**.

How to do it…

So, how do we filter by the dimension(s) available in Explore? When Standard users (Creators) want to create their Looks (visualizations) in Explores based on filtered data, they can use filters, advanced filters, filter groups, and custom expressions. Let's discover these filter options through the following steps:

1. **Basic filters**: To add filters to an Explore, you can click on the upside-down pyramid icon near the dimension you want to filter on (*Figure 3.5*).

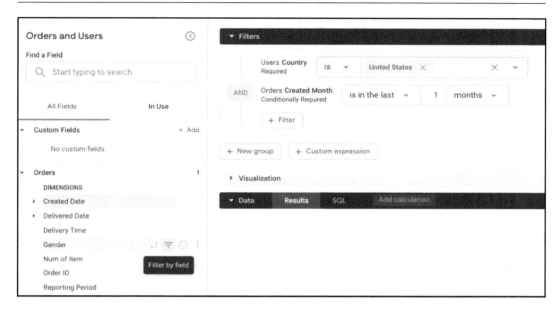

Figure 3.5 – Filter by field

2.   Once added, the filter will provide you with various choices of filter operators – **is**, **contains**, **is null**, and so on. These operators might be different for text and numeric values (*Figure 3.6*).

Figure 3.6 – Filter expressions

3. In the **Orders and Users** Explore, apply the following:

I. Add the **Gender is F** filter (when clicking inside the filter's empty cell, you will see that Looker suggests the possible values for this field).

II. Add the **Num of Items is >= 2** filter.

III. For your `Results` table, choose the column User ID.

IV. Click the **RUN** filter.

V. You will obtain the female users from the US (our default filter configured in LookML) who bought at least two items in the last month (our conditional filter that can't be deleted if we don't filter by user ID).

4. Filters can be added by clicking on the gear icon near the column name in the **Results** tab (*Figure 3.7*).

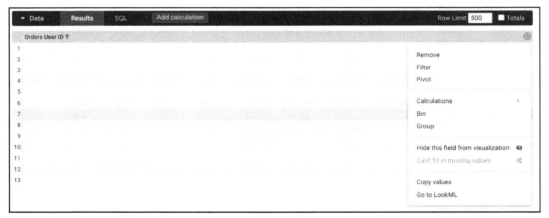

Figure 3.7 – Filter in the Results tab

Basic filters work the same way as measures.

5. **Advanced filters** (**RegEx**): When you choose matches (advanced) as a filter's operator, you can apply advanced filter expressions to it. The advanced filter expressions are quite similar to regular expressions if you've worked with RegEx. Perform the following steps:

I. Delete our previous filters (keep only those added in the LookML; you won't be able to delete them in the Explore user interface) and add the filter by the City dimension.

II. Choose the "matches(advanced)" operator, and for a condition, add the following – `Chi%,-Chicago`.

III. For the `Results` table, choose two columns, `User ID` and `City` (to remove all the previously used columns, click on the gear icon near the column name in the **Results** section).

IV.   Click **Run.**

V.   You will get the users who are from a city that starts with Chi but not Chicago.

The advanced filter has a huge number of different expressions that you can use to customize your filters perfectly. The link on the list of possible expressions is available at the end of this section. String filter matches depend on case-sensitivity settings in your model and dialect. For example, if case sensitivity is enabled, CHI will not match chino.

You might have noticed that Looker transformed your advanced filter to multiple regular filters, creating a new filter group. Let's discover what it is:

- **Filter groups**: A filter group is just a combination of multiple filters connected with the AND or OR operator. OR is used when the result is provided if at least one of the filters is met. AND is used when the result is only given when both filters are met. When you applied the advanced filter, it was transformed into two filters – a city starts with Chi or a city that is not Chicago. To create a filter group, you need to click +**New Group** in the **Filters** section.

- **Custom expressions**: Custom expressions let you create your own filter formula that can use multiple dimensions and measures. The response of the expression should be *yes* or *no* – you will obtain the result in your table for the rows that answer *yes* to your filter expression. Let's do the following to test this:

    I.   In the **Filters** section in the Explore environment, delete the previous filters (except for those you cannot delete).

    II.   Click **Custom expression** and add the following code – add_days(2,${orders. created_date})<${orders.delivered_date}.

    III. Choose the User Id, Created date, and Delivery date columns.

    IV.   Click **Run**.

    V.   The idea of this filter is to check whether we have users that have waited more than two days before they created the order and received it.

Custom expressions give you the highest possible level of customization for your filters. Filtering with measures works the same as filtering with dimensions.

See also

- For more on how to work with filters, visit https://cloud.google.com/looker/docs/filtering-and-limiting, and for more on how to work with advanced filters, visit https://cloud.google.com/looker/docs/filter-expressions.

- For more about Looker functions and operators, visit https://cloud.google.com/looker/docs/functions-and-operators.

Custom fields

If the existing dimensions and measures are not enough for Explore users (Standard users/Creators), they can easily create their custom fields.

Note that custom fields offer temporary, Explore-specific calculations with limited reusability, while LookML provides permanent, model-wide definitions for reusable and governed metrics.

There are multiple ways to create custom fields , and we will go through them in this section. We'll continue working in the **Orders and Users** Explore.

If necessary, you can always prevent users from creating custom fields in Explores (creating custom fields requires the "create_custom_fields" permission assigned by your Looker admin).

How to do it...

To create a custom field, let's do the following:

1. Click on the **Custom Field** section on the left of the Explore environment.

2. Click **+Add**, and you will see three available options – **Custom Dimension**, **Custom Measure**, and **Table Calculation**. Custom fields (dimensions and measures) will generate SQL that will run against the database (such as a LookML-defined field). Table calculations are user-created, temporary calculations executed after the query on the resulting data. The **Table Calculation** option will be available only if there are fields in the **Results** section (if you have already selected columns for your future `results` table).

3. Click on **Custom Dimension**.

4. In the **Expression** cell, add the following code:

   ```
   concat(${users.street_address}," ",${users.postal_code},"
   ",${users.city}," ",${users.country})
   ```

5. Name the dimension `Full Address`, keep the default formatting, and add a description if needed.

6. Click **Save**.

Creating custom fields based on measures

Now, let's create a custom field based on measure:

1. In the **Custom Fields** section in the Explore, click **+Add**.

2. Choose **Custom Measure**.

3. Choose the field to measure – `Num of Item`.

4. Choose the **Measure** type – **Max**. The idea here is to get a maximum number of items bought (for any chosen dimension).

5. You have the possibility to add filters, but we won't do so in this exercise.

6. Click **Save**.

7. Verify whether our newly created dimension, **Full Address**, and **Max Num of Item** work: click **Full Address** and then on Max Num of Item; make sure they are added to the **Results** tab/section.

8. Click **Run**.

9. Check the result – we should get the maximum number of items bought by address (*Figure 3.8*).

Figure 3.8 – Custom fields

Creating Table Calculations

Now, let's add the third type of custom field – **Table Calculation**:

1. In the **Custom Fields** section in the Explore, click +**Add**.

2. Choose **Table Calculation**.

3. Under **Calculation**, choose **Custom expression**.

4. In the Expression cell, add the following code:

```
${max_number_of_items}/sum(${max_number_of_items})
```

5. Under **Format**, choose **Percent**.

6. Name your new custom field `% of Total`. Click **Save**.

   We have created an additional field that calculates the percentage of the maximum number of items in the total amount of maximum items per address. The table calculation takes only the active fields (the columns in the **Results** section), so we worked with what was available to us.

If you want to edit, delete, or duplicate your custom dimension or measure, click on the three dots near the dimension/measure name in the **Custom Fields** section.

Other ways to create custom fields

There are other ways to create custom fields in the Explore, such as the following:

1. **Create a filtered measure**:

   I.   Click on the three dots near the `Count` measure.

   II.   Choose `Count` as the field to measure.

   III. Provide a name – `Users.count (received the order)`.

   IV.   In the `Filters` section under the field name, find the delivery date, and under the **Filter** value, choose **is not null**.

   V.   Check the options available in the field details, but don't change anything.

   VI.   Note the possibility of doing a custom filter as well.

   VII. Click **Save**. We have created a custom measure that counts only users who received their order (the delivery date is available). This measure is now available in the **Custom Fields** section.

   VIII. In the **Results** section, remove all the columns (click on the gear icon near the column in the table and click **Remove**).

   IX.   Click on the `City` and `Users.count (received the order)` columns in the left panel in your **Orders and Users** Explore.

   X.   Click **Run**.

   XI.   Add the `Count` measure and click **Run** again. Compare the number of users (*Figure 3.9*).

Figure 3.9 – A filtered measure

2. **Aggregate**:

 I.   Click on the three dots near the **City** dimension in the left panel.

 II. Click **Aggregate**, and you will then see two options – **Count distinct** and **List of unique values** (you will see more options available for the **Dimensions** number type).

 III. If you click **Count distinct**, it will create a new measure that counts the number of distinct cities.

 IV. If you click **List of unique values**, it will create a new measure as well – List of City.

 V.   In the **Results** section, remove all the columns from the table.

 VI. Choose the Country column on your left, and then choose the newly created List of City column.

 VII. Once the columns have been added to the **Results** section, click **Run**.

You will see one line with United States, and in the List of City column, you will see a list of cities separated by commas. We have only one country because of the default filter created in LookML.

3. **Group**:

 I.   Click on the three dots near the **City** dimension in the left panel

 II. Click **Group**. Here, we can create the dimension that will group values by defined criteria.

 III. Under the field name, add your new dimension's name – City name starts with.

IV.   Under the group name, add four groups by clicking on +; the group names are A, B, C, and Others (*Figure 3.10*).

V.   Click **Save**.

VI.   Remove all the previous columns from the **Results** section, and add your newly created City name starts with and Count (from the Orders table).

VII. Click **Run**.

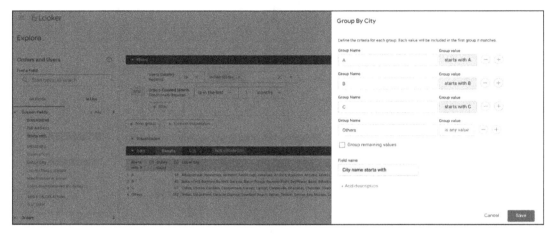

Figure 3.10 – A filtered measure

4. **Bin**:

I.   Click on the three dots near the age dimension.

II.   Click on **Bin**.

III. For bin size, enter 10 (this means the data range will be divided into segments of width 10). Set the minimum value to 0 and the maximum value to 100.

IV.   Name the field New Age Groups.

V.   Click **Save**.

VI.   In the **Results** section, remove all the columns from the table.

VII. Choose the New Age Groups column on your left in the Custom Fields, and then choose Count from the Orders table.

VIII. Click **Run**.

IX.   See the result – we now have a number of orders per age group.

See also

- For more on how to work with custom fields, visit `https://cloud.google.com/looker/docs/custom-fields`, and for more on how to work with Looker expressions, visit `https://cloud.google.com/looker/docs/creating-looker-expressions`.

Pivoting and table manipulations in Explores

Pivoting a dimension to display it horizontally improves the visual comparison of several dimensions at once. Each value in the pivoted dimension becomes a column in the Look, making the information more visually appealing and reducing the need to scroll down to find data. Looker supports up to 200 pivoted values.

How to do it...

Let's discover pivoting in Looker through the following steps:

1. Make sure you are in the Explore environment in the **Orders and Users** Explore.
2. When you hover over any dimension in the left panel of the Explore, you will see an icon with two arrows. Hover over this icon to see the **Pivot Data** text.
3. Click on the **Pivot Data** icon near **Gender**.
4. Then, add an `Age Group` column (from `Users`) and a `Count` column (from `Orders`).
5. Click **Run**. You will see the table that shows a repartition per gender and age group.
6. Click on the **Visualization** section to open it (above the **Results** section). There will be a column visualization added automatically that shows the orders per gender and age group. Through this visualization, we can immediately see that most of the orders were placed by women from 45 to 55 (*Figure 3.11*).

Figure 3.11 – A pivot table

There are various other ways to interact with a table in Explore. The gear icon (⚙) near the column in the `Results` table gives you the possibility to do the following:

- Remove columns

- Filter by a specific column

- Pivot

- Group (like we did for the **New Age Groups** dimension in the previous section)

- Hide the column from the visualization

- Hide the field from the visualization. Try clicking on **Hide** the field from visualization near **Orders Count** in the F column – it will make all the data disappear from the visualization. Now, try clicking on **Show** this field in the visualization, and then click on **Hide this column from the visualization**. This will hide only this specific F column, as we will concentrate on the M data in our visualization.

- Fill in the missing values (will add null values if no data is returned)

- Copy values (this will copy values from the rows)

- Go to LookML

- Calculations (available for measures)
- Create a filtered measure (available for measures)

Above the `Results` table in the **Results** bar, you have options to do the following:

- Increase the row limit (up to 5,000 at the time of writing)
- Show totals and row totals
- Set a column limit

See also

- For more on data exploration in Looker, visit `https://cloud.google.com/looker/docs/creating-and-editing-explores?hl=en`.

Editing visualizations

When working with visualizations in Looker, you have the possibility to use the existing ones, add additional visualizations from Looker Marketplace, and develop and then add your own custom visualizations (adding happens in the **Admin** panel) as well.

You can edit the visualizations in the Explore to make them more clear, beautiful, organized, and readable for your audience.

Getting ready

Make sure you are in your **Orders and Users** Explore. We can continue working with the `Results` table from the previous section that has the `Age Group` and `Gender` columns and is pivoted by gender (*Figure 3.11*). Make sure the **Visualizations** section is open and that the visualization looks like the one we have in *Figure 3.11*.

How to do it...

To edit our existing column-type/bar chart visualization, you need to do the following:

1. In the **Visualization** section, click on **Edit** (near **Forecast**).
2. You will see multiple tabs:

    I.   Go to the **Plot** tab:

        i.   In the **Plot** tab in **Series Positioning**, click **Stacked** and then **Stacked Percentage**. Keep one of the three options based on your preference. Depending on what you keep, other options in the **Plot** tab will change as well.

ii.   Go through the other options, and hide the legend or place it in the center; if you chose **Grouped** under **Series Positioning**, add 0.1 under **Inner Space**, and note what changes are made to the chart. Add 0.5 under **Spacing** to regulate the distance between age groups in the visualization.

iii. Because our two rows in the table don't contain any data, click on **Limit Displayed Rows**, and hide the last two rows.

II.   Then, go to **Series**:

i.   In Colors in Collection, change it to Degree's palette, and then click reverse colors.

ii. Under **Labels**, click on **Show Full Field Name**.

iii. Under **Customizations**, play around with the type – note what changes.

III.   Click on the **Values** tab:

i.   Toggle the **Value** labels to see the number of orders per gender and age group in the visualization.

ii. Change the font size to 14 px.

iii. Change Value Rotation to 300.

iv. Change Value Format to 0.0.

IV.   Go to the **X** tab:

i.   Leave the scale type as it is (the **Time** option is not available for our data, as there is no Time field; the **Ordinal Scale** type doesn't change anything in our case).

ii. Toggle **Show Axis Name** and **Axis Value Labels** to hide them.

V.   Go to the **Y** tab:

i.   Toggle the gridlines to hide them.

ii. Drag and drop the order count from **Left Axes** to **Right Axes**.

iii. Toggle **Show Axis Name** and **Show Axis Values** to hide them.

iv. In **Markings**, click on **Add Reference Line**, and change **Type** to **Range**.

v.   Change the color to blue under **Palettes**.

VI.   Close **Edit** (*Figure 3.12*).

Figure 3.12 – The visualization edit

The tabs might be different, depending on what type of visualization you work with. The tabs listed in the preceding list are specific to the bar chart visualization.

If you scroll the first tab, you will see the **Advanced Editing** option as well – it will give you the possibility to customize the chart JSON.

When you've finished with your visualization's edits, click on **X** near the **Edit** button to close the editing window

Creating Line visualization

For an additional example, let's choose different data and a different visualization type and then edit it:

1. First of all, let's go back to our LookML environment and the LookML model (click on **Go to LookML** in the bottom-left corner if you're in Development Mode).

2. In the `lb_thelook_ecommerce.model` model file in the `orders_and_users` Explore, delete `conditionally_filter` to not limit our data to the last month. In the lb_thelook_ecommerce.model model file in the orders_and_users Explore, delete conditionally_filter to not limit our data to the last month:

   ```
   conditionally_filter: {
     filters: [orders.created_month: "1 month"]
     unless: [users.id]
   }
   ```

3. Click **Save Changes**.

4. Above the code editor window, click on the arrow icon near the `lb_thelook_ecommerce.`
    `model` model name, and then choose the **Orders and Users** Explore.

5. Now, let's work in the Explore environment. Choose the `Delivered Month` column
    (`Delivered Date | Month`) and the `Count` column from `Orders`. We want to know
    how many orders we had per month for all the period of our activity (or the data availability).

6. Click **Run**.

7. In the **Visualization** tab, choose **Line visualization**.

8. You will see that months repeat; this is because we have multiple years in our data. Let's add a
    filter to limit our data to the year 2022.

9. In the `Results` table, click on the gear icon near the `Delivered Month` column, and then
    click **Filter**. Choose **is in the year** as the filter operator, and add 2022 as a value,

10. Click **Run** again.

11. Click **Edit** in the **Visualization** section.

12. Under **Series in Point Style**, click **Filled**.

13. Under **Values**, toggle **Value Labels** to show the values.

14. Under **Y**, toggle **Gridlines** to hide them.

15. Under **Y**, toggle **Show Axis Values**.

16. Click **Edit** (*Figure 3.13*).

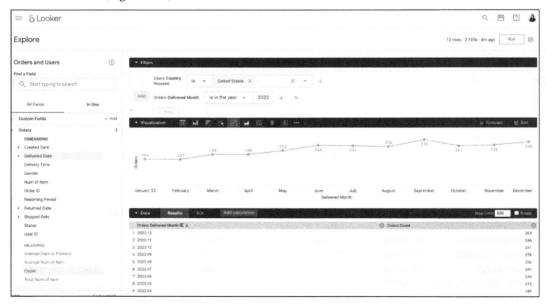

Figure 3.13 – The line visualization

Every visualization type has a lot of parameters that you can modify to make it perfect for your dashboard. Try other types of visualizations to see the edit options available.

There's more...

Selecting the right type of visualization is very important and, sometimes, a slightly complicated task. Here are some factors to consider when selecting the right visualization type:

- **The type of data you have**: Some visualizations are better suited for certain types of data than others. For example, line charts are good for showing trends over time, while bar charts are good for comparing categories.

- **The purpose of your visualization**: What do you want your audience to understand from the data? Are you trying to show trends, relationships, or comparisons?

- **The audience for your visualization**: Who will be viewing your visualization? What is their level of data literacy?

- **The context in which your visualization will be used**: Will it be used in a presentation, a report, or on a website?

Your visualization has an essential role – to convey a narrative in a clear and concise manner. We use a visualization to facilitate the communication of data-driven insights. Here are some tips to create a great visualization:

- **Keep it simple**: The simpler your visualization, the easier it will be for your audience to understand.

- **Use clear and concise labels**: Make sure that your labels are easy to read and understand.

- **Avoid cluttering your visualization**: Too much data can make your visualization difficult to understand.

- **Use color effectively**: Color can be used to highlight important data or show relationships between data.

- **Test your visualization with others**: Get feedback from others on your visualization to make sure that it is clear and easy to understand.

You can find the Looker guide on selecting the right visualization here: `https://cloud.google.com/looker/docs/visualization-guide`.

See also

- For more on working with visualizations, visit `https://cloud.google.com/looker/docs/creating-visualizations`, and for more on different visualization types, visit `https://cloud.google.com/looker/docs/visualization-types`.

- For more on the **Forecast** option, visit `https://cloud.google.com/looker/docs/forecasting-in-visualizations`.

Merging data from multiple Explores

Explores are usually designed and prepared by dedicated LookML developers in your team (usually data engineers) and contain data from one or more tables, with a defined relationship between these tables. It is advised to use a prepared Explore to analyze the data.

However, data analysts and other Looker Explorers might need to combine data from multiple Explores in cases that were not predicted by LookML developers, and in this scenario, merged results can help you. They allow you to combine results from different Explores (even from different models, projects, or even connections) for exploration and visualization.

This powerful technique can be used as a test for further LookML development. It can be used as a proof of concept for your future LookML projects and models.

> **Important note**
> Merged results, a post-query processing feature, can strain Looker instance resources and slow down response times for all users if not used judiciously.

Getting ready

1. Make sure you are in your Explore environment, in the **Orders and Users** Explore.

2. Unpivot the source query (as it is impossible to perform a merge on pivoted Explores).

3. Remove all the existing columns from the `Results` table.

4. Choose `City` from the `Users` and `Count` columns from the `Orders` table, and then click **Run**.

Analyzing the results, you want to understand not only what cities the users who placed orders come from but also what traffic source brings them to your website. We may realize that we want to add information about the traffic source that is not in our **Orders and Users** Explore, but in the **Event** Explore instead. We'll need to use the merge results functionality for that.

How to do it...

To merge Explores, complete the following steps:

1. Click on the gear icon near the **Run** button.

2. Choose **Merge Results**.

3. In the left panel of the pop-up window, you will see different Explores available. If you have multiple projects, you will see the Explores from all these projects.

4. Find the **Events** Explore; click on it. This Explore contains columns from the Events and Users tables.

5. Choose the columns you'll need from the **Events** explore – City (from Users) and Traffic Source. Click **Run**, and then, in the top-right corner, click **Save**.

6. The **Merged Results** window will open, and under **MERGE RULES**, make sure you connect the Explores by the Users.City field.

7. Click **Run**.

8. In the gear icon near the **Run** button, you have the possibility to save your merged Explore to the dashboard (when you click on **Save to Dashboard**, there will be an option to create a new one or reuse an existing one – *Figure 3.14*).

9. In the same **Merged Results** window, you have the possibility to go back to your **Orders and Users** or **Events** Explores and edit them if needed (*Figure 3.14*).

Figure 3.14 – The pivot table

How it works...

When merging, your first Explore (**Orders and Users** in our case) is considered as a primary query. Looker will merge the results of each added query with the primary query, using the specified common dimension. Merged results work similarly to a left join.

Merged results have a limit of 5,000 rows per query.

Fields from the primary query take precedence over those from added queries. If there is a name conflict between the two, the primary query's name will be used.

See also

- For more on merged Explores, visit `https://cloud.google.com/looker/docs/merged-results`.

Sharing Explores

You know already that to share your work in LookML, you need to push changes to your git environment. But what about Explores? Explores are created in LookML, and access to them can be managed in LookML through different access restrictions (using `access_filter` parameter) or the **Users** section in the **Admin** panel (**Admin**->**Users**->**Roles**). When the Explores are shared, they usually have the same set of columns available (unless you prevent some users from seeing some column or rows in LookML). All the changes that Creators (Explore users) make can be saved as a Look (basically, a visualization unit based on a combination of columns, filters, and customized columns, created by the Explore user/Creator).

In Looker, you can also easily share customized data views with colleagues by sharing the Explore URL. When someone uses that shared URL, they'll instantly see the Explore you created, complete with all the filters, dimensions, and measures you've already applied.

How to do it...

Let's discover multiple sharing options in Explores:

1. If you click on the gear icon (⚙) near the **Run** button, you can save your visualization as a Look, to an existing dashboard or as a new Dashboard (the latter option will still create a Look but add it immediately to a newly created Dashboard).

2. In the same place, by clicking on the gear icon, you can download your work as CSV, text, JSON, HTML, Markdown, or PNG and choose different options, such as the results, data values, and number of rows and columns to include. Once downloaded, it can be sent to the destination person.

3. You can also see the **Share** option in the list, accessible by clicking the gear icon near the **Run** button); this option gives you the possibility to share the URL of your Explore work. The person you share your URL with should have access to Looker space.

4. The **Send** option in the list gives you quite a lot of possibilities to share your work (some should be activated in the Looker Action Hub to appear):

    *   Email
    *   Webhook
    *   Amazon S3
    *   SFTP
    *   Facebook Custom Audiences
    *   Firebase
    *   Google Ads Customer Match
    *   Google Analytics Data Import
    *   Google Cloud Storage
    *   Google Drive
    *   Google Sheets
    *   JIRA
    *   Marketo
    *   SendGrid
    *   Slack
    *   Teams – Incoming Webhook
    *   Zapier
    *   Update Contact in Hubspot
    *   Salesforce Campaigns [BETA]
    *   Vertex AI

    (Other options might be added soon.) These options give you the possibility to share your work with your colleagues and partners through third-party tools, as well as to continue working with your prepared and filtered data in advertising, email, and AI/ML spaces.

5. **Get embed URL** gives you the possibility to embed your visualization. Click on **Get embed URL** and copy the embed URL. You can paste the URL into a new browser window or tab to preview the embedded content. You can also use this URL to embed the content in an *iframe*. There'll be more on embedding later in this book.

There's more...

You might have seen the **Get LookML** option in the list when clicking on the gear icon (⚙) near the **Run** button. This option gives you three possibilities:

- **Dashboard**: Getting a LookML for a visualization gives you the possibility to add it to your existing LookML dashboard. A LookML dashboard is a collection of visualizations created using LookML, Looker's data modeling language. LookML dashboards are stored as version-controlled files, making them easy to manage and share. They offer advantages over user-defined dashboards, such as reusability, maintainability, dynamism, and consistency.

- **Aggregate Table**: It is possible to get LookML code to create an Explore in the model, based on the aggregate table. In Looker, an aggregate table is a pre-calculated summary of data. Aggregate tables are created using the `aggregate_table` parameter in LookML. When a query is run against an Explore that has an associated aggregate table, Looker will automatically use the aggregate table if it is a good fit for the query. This can significantly improve the performance of queries, especially for large datasets. Aggregate tables can be a valuable tool to improve the performance of Looker queries. However, it is important to carefully consider the pros and cons of using aggregate tables before creating them.

- **Derived Table**: It is possible to get a LookML code to create a view in the LookML project, based on the derived table. A derived table in Looker is a temporary or persistent table that is created by running a query. Derived tables can be used to pre-calculate complex or frequently used calculations, join data from multiple sources, create temporary tables for use in LookML code, or create **persistent derived tables** (**PDTs**) that are stored in a database and refreshed on a schedule. Derived tables can be a valuable tool to improve the performance and usability of Looker. However, it is important to carefully consider the pros and cons of using derived tables before creating them.

See also

- For more on aggregate tables, visit `https://cloud.google.com/looker/docs/reference/param-explore-aggregate-table`.

- Read more about sharing your Looker content here: `https://cloud.google.com/looker/docs/send-and-share-content`.

4
Customizing and Serving Dashboards

A Looker dashboard is a single page that combines multiple visualizations and data elements into a single, interactive view. Dashboards allow you to see all of your most important data in one place, and to easily filter and explore that data to answer your questions.

Tiles are the individual building blocks of Looker dashboards. Tiles can contain any type of visualization, such as tables, charts, images, markdown, button and text. You can also add filters to your dashboard to control which data is displayed in the tiles. Once you have added tiles to your dashboard, you can arrange them in any way you like. You can also resize and customize the tiles to match your needs.

When you are finished building your dashboard, you can share it with others in your organization. Looker dashboards can be shared via email, links, or embedded in other applications.

Looker dashboards are a powerful tool for data visualization and analysis. They can help you to get a better understanding of your data and to make more informed decisions.

Here are some examples of how Looker dashboards can be used:

- A sales team can use a dashboard to track their sales performance by region, product, and customer type.

- A marketing team can use a dashboard to track the performance of their marketing campaigns by channel, campaign type, and audience.

- A customer support team can use a dashboard to track the volume and severity of customer support tickets.

- A product team can use a dashboard to track the usage and engagement of their product.

Looker dashboards can be used for a variety of other purposes as well. The possibilities are endless.

In this chapter, we're going to cover the following recipes:

- Adding visualizations to dashboards
- Adding text and markdown to dashboards
- Working with buttons in dashboards
- Filtering and cross-filtering in dashboards
- Working with settings in dashboards
- Moving, editing, and deleting tiles

Technical requirements

There are no specific requirements or preparation steps for this chapter; we will continue working with our **thelook_ecommerce** dataset: `https://console.cloud.google.com/marketplace/product/bigquery-public-data/thelook-ecommerce`, switching between Explore and Dashboard environments inside Looker. We won't be working in BigQuery (which is the data warehouse used in this book) as we assume our dataset is already connected to Looker and ready to be used in it. But you can keep the **BigQuery** tab open to preview the tables and get familiarized with the data you'll be exploring in Looker.

Adding visualizations to dashboards

In the previous chapters, we have already explored how to create a dashboard from **Explore**: you first need to create your Look (visualization) in **Explore**, then you click on the gear ⚙ icon near the **Run** button and choose **Save** -> **As a new dashboard** (*Figure 4.1*).

As a reminder, a **Look** in Looker is a saved analysis (query result) or visualization that provides insights into your data. It is a single, reusable building block that can be combined with other Looks to create dashboards and to be shared with users.

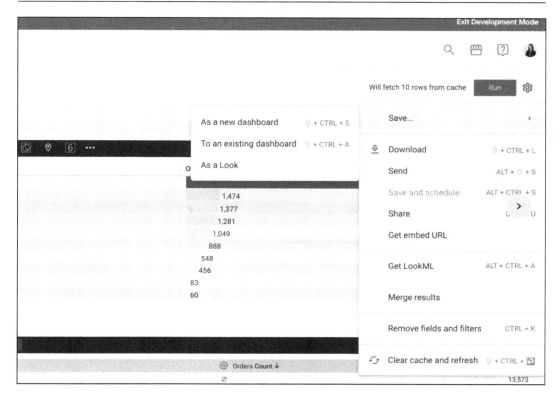

Figure 4.1 – Create dashboard from Explore

You can save your Explore analysis (visualization) as a Look or add it directly to a new or existing dashboard (*Figure 4.2*). Later, you can add other elements called **tiles** to your dashboard. Tiles can be visualizations (based on Looks or created specifically for the dashboard) or text. How do we add elements to the dashboard directly from the tile dashboard interface?

Getting ready

Go to the **Home** page by clicking on the Looker logo or by going to (*add your instance URL*)/browse. Then go to **Folders** -> **My folder** (*Figure 4.2*).

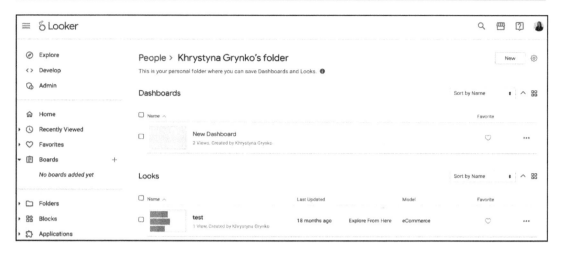

Figure 4.2 – My folder

If you followed the previous chapters, you'll probably have some elements there already, such as dashboards or Looks.

How to do it...

To create a dashboard, you need to do the following:

1. In **My folder,** click on **New** (near the gear icon in the top-right corner) and choose **Dashboard.**

2. In the small pop-up window that appears, give your dashboard a name (for example, Ecommerce Dashboard), then click on **Create Dashboard.** You should now see an empty dashboard page.

3. Click on **Edit Dashboard.**

4. Click on **Add -> Visualization.**

5. In the pop-up **Explore** window that appears, search for our **Orders and Users** Explore and click on it.

6. In the **Edit Tile** interface that appears, you can create a visualization as you have done in the regular **Explore** interface.

7. Choose the **Age Group** from Users and **Count** from Orders columns to have the number of orders per age group and click **Run.**

8. Sort the **Orders Count** column by descending order by clicking on it in the **Results** tab. The two last rows will be empty (no data for these age groups).

9. In the **Visualization** section, choose the **Bar** type of visualization, and in the right corner, click on **Edit.**

10. In the **Edit** section of **visualization**, click on the **Plot** tab and scroll until you see the **Limit Displayed Rows** option – toggle it, then configure it to hide the last two rows.

11. Close the **Edit** section by clicking on **X** (*Figure 4.3*).

12. In the top-right corner, click **Save**.

13. The visualization is added to your dashboard.

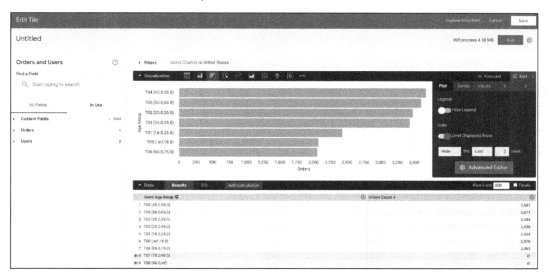

Figure 4.3 – Edit Tile

In the **Edit Tile** interface, you have the possibility to switch to the **Explore** interface by clicking on **Explore from Here** in the top-right corner, near the **Save** and **Cancel** buttons. The **Cancel** button gives you the possibility to cancel the visualization creation process if you change your mind and the **Stop** button can stop the query from running. In the top-left corner, you can change the name of the visualization by clicking on **Untitled**.

There's more...

You can build your dashboard using LookML code. This kind of dashboard is called a LookML dashboard and can be transformed into a regular user-defined dashboard. You'll find a LookML dashboard overview here: `https://cloud.google.com/looker/docs/reference/lookml-dashboard-overview`

See also

- Creating user-defined dashboards: `https://cloud.google.com/looker/docs/creating-user-defined-dashboards`

- Saving and editing Looks: `https://cloud.google.com/looker/docs/saving-and-editing-looks`

Adding text and markdown to dashboards

Text and **Markdown elements** in Looker dashboards are used to add descriptive text, headings, and other formatting to your dashboards.

Text elements provide a simple way to add text to your dashboard. You can use text elements to add titles, subtitles, labels, and other descriptive text.

Markdown elements allow you to use Markdown formatting to add text, headings, links, images, and other content to your dashboard.

Getting ready

We'll continue working in our **Ecommerce Dashboard** where we created a visualization in the previous section.

How to do it...

To add text and markdown elements to your dashboard, you need to do the following:

1. Let's start with adding a text element to your dashboard:

   I. In the top-left corner of **Ecommerce Dashboard**, click on **Add** -> then choose **Text**.

   II. The text at the top will be the heading. Add the following there: `This is an Ecommerce website dashboard.`

   III. Below the heading, add any description text, such as, for example, `TheLook is a fictitious eCommerce clothing site developed by the Looker team. The dataset contains information about customers, products, orders, logistics, web events, and digital marketing campaigns. The contents of this dataset are synthetic and are provided to industry practitioners for the purpose of product discovery, testing, and evaluation.`

2. To add a markdown element to your dashboard, you need to do the following:

   I. In the top-left corner of **Ecommerce Dashboard**, click on **Add**, then choose **Markdown**.

   II. In **Title**, you can add the following: `To know more about Looker go to ->.`

III.   In the **Body** section, add the following: `[Looker Doc] (https://www.looker.com)`.

IV.   Click **Save**.

3.   By clicking in the bottom-right corner of the tile, you can reduce its size.

4.   By clicking in the top-right corner, on the three dots, you can edit the tile, delete it, move it, duplicate it, and view it in expanded or fullscreen mode.

5.   By clicking in the top-left corner, you can move your tiles.

6.   Let's add a logo to our dashboard:

I.   In the top-right corner of the previous tile (**To know more about Looker go to ->**), click on three dots, then click on **Edit**.

II.   In the body, add the following: `<img src="https://upload.wikimedia.org/wikipedia/commons/thumb/4/4c/Looker.svg/2560px-Looker.svg.png">`.

III.   Click **Save**.

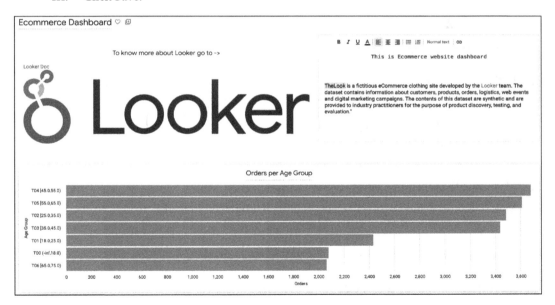

Figure 4.4 – Dashboard with text and markdown

7.   You can move and resize the tiles as you wish. Try to make something like shown on the screen in *Figure 4.4*.

8.   In the top-right corner of your dashboard, click **Save** to save all your changes to your dashboard.

See also

- Learn more about the Markdown here: `https://cloud.google.com/looker/docs/using-markdown-in-text-tiles`

- About Markdown Document Navigation, from the Looker community: `https://www.googlecloudcommunity.com/gc/Modeling/Markdown-Document-Navigation/td-p/566469`

Working with buttons in dashboards

Buttons in Looker dashboards are interactive elements that allow users to perform actions, such as navigating to a different report, for example, or to the documentation page.

Getting ready

We'll continue working in our **Ecommerce Dashboard** dashboard (in Edit Mode) where we created one visualization and text and Markdown elements.

How to do it...

Here's how to add a button to a dashboard using the Looker UI:

1. In the top-left corner of **Ecommerce Dashboard**, click on **Add**, then choose **Button**.
2. For the label, add the following text: `Go to the website`.
3. For the link, add the following URL: `https://cloud.google.com/looker`.
4. Leave the description empty for now. This description will appear when you hover over the button (if empty, the description defaults to the link).
5. Make sure the **Open in a new browser tab** option is selected.
6. Make color, size, and alignment changes in the **Design** tab if needed.
7. Click **Save**
8. You can move and resize buttons on the dashboard as needed.

Filtering and cross-filtering in dashboards

We've already explored the filtering in LookML that limits what **Explore** users see and how they can interact with data.

Filtering in Looker dashboards allows viewer-type users to limit the data that is displayed in dashboard tiles. This can be useful for focusing the analysis on a specific subset of data or for hiding data that is not relevant to the current task. Dashboard filters can either impact all tiles on the dashboard or be targeted to individual tiles for more granular control.

The **Filters** section in the top-left corner of the dashboard in edit mode gives the possibilities to do the following:

- Add filters.

- Toggle the **Cross-filtering** option. Cross-filtering is a feature that allows you to filter the data in one tile by clicking on data points in another tile. However, merged results visualizations from different Explores are incompatible with dashboard-level cross-filters.

- Toggle the **Apply filter edits to alerts** option. The **Apply filter edits to alerts** toggle in Looker dashboards allows you to sync changes made to dashboard filters with all alerts on the dashboard. This means that if you edit a dashboard filter, any alerts that are associated with that dashboard will be automatically updated to reflect the new filter settings.

Getting ready

We'll continue working in our **Ecommerce Dashboard** dashboard (in Edit Mode) where we created a visualization, text, Markdown, and button elements.

How to do it...

To add a filter to a dashboard, take the following steps:

1. In the top-left corner of the dashboard, in edit mode, click on **Filters -> Add Filter**.

2. In the available **Orders and Users Explore**, choose the dimension or measure you want to filter on. (If you toggle **Advanced**, you can search for a dimension or a measure with all the models and Explores.)

3. In **Orders and Users**, choose **Orders -> Delivered Date -> Delivered Year**.

4. Keep the title as it is.

5. In the **Control** section, choose **Advanced**.

6. In **Configure Default Value**, choose **is in the year 2023**.

7. The **Allow multiple filter values** option gives the possibility to have the **OR operator** in the filter. Let's uncheck this for now.

8. In **Tiles To Update** tab, make no changes – at this stage, we have only one visualization so there's no need to specify this.

9. In the bottom-right corner of the **Add Filter** window, click on **Add** to save your filter.

10. Position the filter on the dashboard and move it if needed.

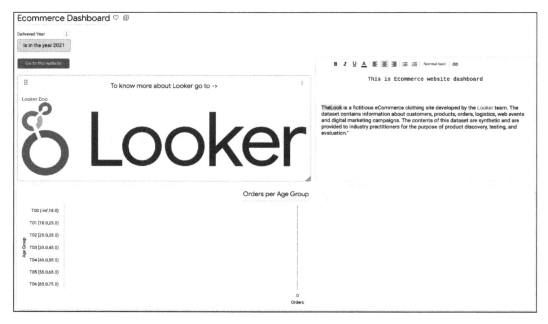

Figure 4.5 – Dashboard filters

11. On the dashboard, try updating the filter value to 2021 and click on **Update** in the top-right corner – the bars will disappear from the visualization as we have no data for the year 2021 (*Figure 4.5.*) or it was filtered in LookML.

12. Before adding another filter, let's add another visualization. In the top-left corner, click on **Add -> Visualization**.

13. Search for **Orders and Users explore**.

14. Choose the **Country** dimension from **Users** – you will see that the data is limited to United States because we enforced the filter for our users. Let's change it:

   I.   In the bottom-left corner, click on **Go to LookML** (available if you have **Development mode** activated) – this will open a new tab.

   II.   Go to **lb_thelook_ecommerce.model**.

   III. Find explore: orders_and_users.

IV.   Delete the following code (to remove the country-specific filter within the Explore and to include all countries in the results):

```
always_filter: {
  filters: [
    users.country: "United States"
  ]
}
```

V.   In the LookML editor, in the top-right corner, click **Save Changes**.

15. In the **Edit Tile** section, click on **Cancel** – we will need to repeat our visualization creation process to take into account our model changes.

16. In the top-left corner, click on **Add -> Visualization**.

17. Search for **Orders and Users explore**.

18. Choose the **Country** dimension from **Users** and the **Count** measure from **Orders** (delete the **United States** value from the filter – even if it stays red, the query will still work).

19. Click **Run**.

20. Choose the **Map** visualization.

21. Name the tile Where do our orders come from?.

22. Click on **Save** in the top-right corner of the **Edit Tile** window.

23. Move the tile on the dashboard if needed.

24. So, we have an age-related and country-related visualization. Let's add some gender information to complete our demographics reporting:

I.   In the top-left corner, click on **Add -> Visualization**.

II.   Search for Orders and Users **Orders and Users explore**.

III. Choose the **Gender** dimension from **Users** and the **Count** measure from **Orders**.

IV.   Click **Run**.

V.   Choose **Pie Chart** as the visualization.

VI.   Name the tile **Order per Gender**.

VII. Click **Save** in the top-right corner of the **Edit Tile** window.

25. Let's add another filter to our dashboard:

I.   In the top-left corner, click on **Filters -> Add Filter**.

II.   In the search bar, in the **Add Filter** window, search for Traffic Source.

III. In **Display**, click **Popover**.

Popover filters and inline filters are two different ways to display filters in Looker dashboards. Popover filters are displayed in a separate window that appears when you click on the filter icon. Inline filters are displayed directly in the dashboard tile.

IV.   Leave the other parameters untouched.

V.   Click **Save**.

26. Test your new filter by clicking on it and choosing **Display** as the value (*Figure 4.6*). Don't forget to click on **Update** in the top-right corner of the dashboard to update the data.

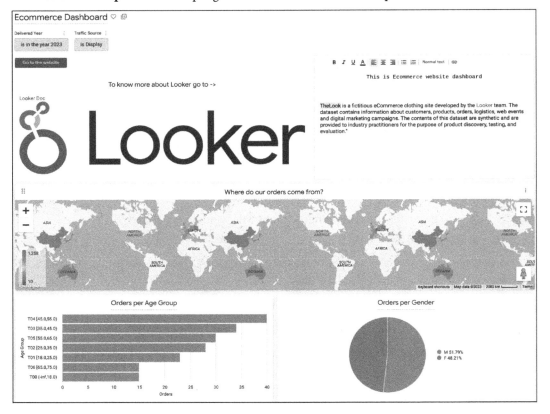

Figure 4.6 – Dashboard traffic source filters

27. When you're happy with your changes, click on **Save** in the top-right corner of the dashboard interface.

See also

- Adding and editing user-defined dashboard filters: `https://cloud.google.com/looker/docs/filters-user-defined-dashboards`

Working with settings in dashboards

Looker dashboards have a variety of settings that you can use to customize the look and feel of your dashboard, as well as to control how users interact with it.

How to do it...

Let's discover the setting options of the dashboard:

1. To access the dashboard settings, open the dashboard in edit mode and click the **Settings** button.
2. In the **General** tab, set **Automatically refresh dashboard every 1 Day**.
3. Let's keep the Refresh frequency "Same as dashboard" for all the tiles
4. In the **Filters** tab, in the **default filters view**, choose **Expanded**, and in **Filters location**, choose **Right**.
5. Click **Save**.
6. In the dashboard interface, click **Save** as well to save all your dashboard change.
7. You might now see the filters on the right part of the page and the data of this dashboard will be refreshed regularly (every day).
8. You may go to **Settings** again to play with different configurations.

How it works...

Looker dashboard filters can be displayed in either **Expanded** or **Collapsed mode**.

Expanded mode displays all the filter options in a single, expanded window. This can be helpful for filters with a lot of options, or for filters that users need to be able to see all the options at once.

Collapsed mode keeps the filter options in a collapsed window. When the filter is collapsed, users can click on the filter icon to expand the window and view the filter options. This can be helpful for filters that are not used frequently, or for filters that users do not need to see all the options for at once.

The **Run on load** setting in Looker dashboards determines whether the data in the dashboard tiles is automatically reloaded when the dashboard is loaded. This setting is enabled by default for new dashboards. For existing dashboards, you can enable or disable it by opening the dashboard in edit mode and clicking the **Settings** button.

There are a few things to keep in mind when using the **Run on load** setting:

- If the dashboard contains a lot of data, reloading the data on load can take some time.
- If the dashboard contains data that changes frequently, enabling **Run on load** will ensure that users are always seeing the most up-to-date data. However, the overall freshness of data will still depend on the caching policy.
- If the dashboard contains data that does not change frequently, disabling **Run on load** can improve the performance of the dashboard.

See also

- Editing user-defined dashboards: `https://cloud.google.com/looker/docs/editing-user-defined-dashboards`

Serving dashboards

In the previous sections, we made different changes to **Ecommerce Dashboard**. Now let's discover how we can share our dashboard with others. Serving dashboards in Looker can be done in several ways:

- Through Looker UI or by sharing the dashboard URL
- By embedding dashboards in other applications
- By scheduling the dashboard delivery by email, webhook etc.

In this section, we'll discover how to share a dashboard with others through the Looker user interface.

Getting ready

The dashboard you saved can always be found in **Folders -> My folder**. When you are in **My folder**, by clicking on the three dots near **Ecommerce Dashboard**, you have the option **Move the dashboard to another folder** (it could be your team's folder) or add it to the board. Boards in Looker provide a way for teams to find curated dashboards and Looks. Dashboards and Looks, which are stored in folders, can be added to multiple boards. This is one of the ways to share your dashboard with Looker users.

How to do it...

If you click on **Ecommerce Dashboard** to open it and then click on the three dots in the top-right corner, there are multiple options to share the dashboard:

1. **Download**: You can download the dashboard in PDF or CSV and send it to a colleague who has, for example, no access to Looker UI by email.
2. **Add to a board**: We already explored this earlier in this section.

3. Get a link to the dashboard to send it to your colleague who has access to the Looker UI.

4. **Get embed URL**: This can be private or signed. An embed URL in Looker is a unique URL that you can use to embed a Looker dashboard in another application. When you embed a dashboard, it appears as an iframe in the other application. We will explore this later in the book.

See also

- Send and share content: `https://cloud.google.com/looker/docs/send-and-share-content`
- *Through the Looker Glass – Part 2: Creating User-Friendly Looker Dashboards with Information Modals*: `https://datatonic.com/insights/creating-user-friendly-looker-dashboards/`

5

Making Dashboards Interactive through Dynamic Elements

In this chapter, we will dive into the art of making your Looker dashboards interactive. Static dashboards provide information, but interactive dashboards empower your users to explore and engage directly with their data. You will learn different techniques to achieve this interaction.

Looker uses Liquid to make Explores and dashboards more interactive. Liquid is a templating language that Looker uses to create dynamic content. It is a powerful tool that allows the creation of complex and personalized experiences for users.

Liquid is a relatively simple language to learn, but it can be very powerful once you master it. It is used in conjunction with LookML to build more flexible, dynamic code.

Liquid is a versatile tool that can be used in Looker for many purposes, including creating dynamic links and images, customizing drill navigation, and applying conditional formatting based on the data. There are several places in LookML where Liquid can be used: the `link` parameter, the HTML parameter, the `label` parameter of a field, the `action` parameter, and parameters that begin with SQL.

In this chapter, we're going to cover the following recipes:

- Working with links
- Working with HTML parameters
- Working with `Liquid` parameters in labels
- Working with dynamic SQL
- Working with actions

Technical requirements

There are no specific requirements or preparation steps for this chapter. We will continue working with our **thelook_ecommerce** dataset (`https://console.cloud.google.com/marketplace/product/bigquery-public-data/thelook-ecommerce`), switching regularly between LookML, Explore, and dashboard environments inside Looker. We won't be working inside BigQuery (which is our data warehouse used in this book) as we assume our dataset is already connected to Looker and ready to be used in it. But you can keep the BigQuery tab open to preview the tables and get familiar with the data you'll be exploring in Looker.

Working with links

The `link` parameter in Looker is a way to create dynamic links to other Looker content and external websites. It takes the following arguments: a `label`, a `URL`, and an `icon_url`. You can use Liquid variables to make the link dynamic, based on the data in your Looker instance.

The `link` parameter can be used to create dynamic links in Looker dashboards. It is a powerful tool that can help you create a more engaging and informative experience for your users. The following are example use cases of the `link` parameter:

- Connect an executive dashboard to a detailed dashboard

- Add a link to an Explore from a Look or dashboard

- Link to a related page on the external web (e.g., a Salesforce page) from a value in a Look or dashboard

- Link to a related page in a different internal system (e.g., an internal application or intranet page) from a value in a Look or dashboard

- Create a custom drill path to explore a dimension or measure in more detail

Getting ready

In this section, we will work in multiple environments: LookML to create the `link` parameter(s), Explore to build a Look with the dimension or measure that contains this `link` parameter, and a dashboard to add the Look into it and see how links work in dashboards. We'll start with the LookML project. If you're on the Looker home page, find the **Develop** tab (usually in the menu on your left), click on it, and then click on **Projects**. On the LookML projects page, find your **lb_thelook_ecommerce** project and click on it.

How to do it...

To add the `link` parameter to your dimension or measure, do the following:

1. In your LookML environment in your **lb_thelook_ecommerce** project, click on **Views** and then open `users view` by clicking on it.

   On our website, people can buy from any country, and we want to provide quickly accessible information to our analysts about these countries. Let's add a link to a Google search.

2. In `users view`, find a country dimension.

3. In the country dimension, after the `SQL` line, click **Enter** and add the following code:

```
link: {
   label: "Google Search"
   url: "http://www.google.com/search?q={{ value }}"
   icon_url: "http://google.com/favicon.ico"
}
```

4. In the top-right corner of the LookML editor, click on **Save Changes** (*Figure 5.1*).

Figure 5.1 – Link parameter in LookML

5. Click on the arrow near `users.view` above the code editor and choose **Explore Users**.

6. In the **Explore** environment, choose **Country** and **Count**.

7. Press **Run**.

8. Note the three-dots icon that appears near the country name. Click on it – you will see the `link` parameter available (*Figure 5.2*).

9. Click on the link to test whether it works.

10. As a visualization, choose **Map**.

11. In the top-right corner, click on the gear icon | **Save** | **Save to an existing dashboard**.

12. In the pop-up window, you can find your dashboard in the **My Folder** section. Choose **Ecommerce Dashboard**, then click **Save to Dashboard**.

Figure 5.2 – Link parameter in Explore

13. You will see the green bar appear with the following message: **"New Tile" has been added to the "Ecommerce Dashboard" Dashboard**. Click on **Ecommerce Dashboard** in this message.

14. You will see two similar map visualizations, but the new one contains the `link` parameter – you might want to delete the old one and replace it with the new one.

15. To edit the dashboard, click on the three dots in the top-right corner of the dashboard, then click on **Edit Dashboard**.

16. If you don't see any data in the dashboard, this might be related to the filters applied to your `orders_and_users` Explore in the model file. Try deleting the following code from your model file in `orders_and_users`:

```
always_filter: {
  filters: [
    users.country: "United States"
  ]
}
conditionally_filter: {
  filters: [orders.created_month: "1 month"]
  unless: [users.id]
}
```

17. Then, click **Save Changes** and go back to your dashboard (refresh the page).

What if we want to give our analysts the possibility to go to a country-dedicated dashboard with the dynamic link? Let's do the following:

1. Go to **Ecommerce Dashboard**.

2. In the top-right corner, click on the three dots and then click on **Copy Dashboard**. Name it `Ecommerce Dashboard (country)`.

3. In this newly created dashboard, delete all the filters and add a filter by country.

4. Note somewhere the number of the dashboard (you can find it in the URL; my number is 1925).

5. Go to LookML, to our country dimension in `users.view`. This dimension already contains a `link` parameter. Let's add the second one (don't forget to replace the 1925 with the number that you can find in your dashboard's URL):

```
link: {
  label: "{{value}} Analytics Dashboard"
  url: "/dashboards/1925?Country={{ value | encode_uri }}"
  #to pass the value of the dimension or measure
}
```

Alternatively, use the following code if you want to take the filter values from the dashboard and pass them into the URL with Liquid:

```
link: {
  label: "{{value}} Analytics Dashboard"
  url: "/dashboards/1925?Country={{_filters['users.country'] |
  url_encode }}"
}
```

6. Save the changes.

7. Go to **Ecommerce Dashboard** and refresh the page.

8. In the map, click on the country (China, for example) – see *Figure 5.3*. You will see the new `link` parameter available: **China Analytics Dashboard**. Click on it, and you will be redirected to the China-dedicated dashboard.

Figure 5.3 – Link parameter in dashboard

Note that in order to make your changes visible to your colleagues, you need to publish LookML changes to a Git environment. For that, you need to do the following:

1. In your LookML editor, click on **Save Changes**.

2. Then, click on **Validate LookML**, correct the errors (if you're not sure how to correct an error at this stage, go to the problematic element and comment it for now with the # symbol). LookML errors are shown in the right panel—**Project Health** (to open this panel click on the **Project Health** icon near **Validate LookML button** and **Quick Help icon** – check *Figure 5.1*). **Project Health** panel provides you with the links to the errors as well.

3. Once you've dealt with the errors, you will see a **No Errors** message appear in the **Project Health** section.

4. In the top-right corner, click on **Commit Changes and Push**.

5. For improved organization, consider moving the dashboard to your team's folder. Check *Chapter 8*.

See also

- More about `link` parameters: `https://cloud.google.com/looker/docs/reference/param-field-link`

Working with HTML parameters

Compared to links, HTML parameters in LookML provide even more possibilities for customized drilling and linking. Here are some examples of how an HTML parameter can be used:

- Creating links to other Looks or external websites
- Adding images and conditional formatting to visualizations
- Creating interactive elements

The HTML parameter is a powerful tool that can be used to create more dynamic and engaging dashboards. However, it is important to note that the HTML parameter is subject to HTML sanitization, which means that certain HTML tags and attributes are not allowed. This is to prevent users from injecting malicious code into your Looker instance.

Getting ready

In this section, we will work in multiple environments: LookML to create the HTML parameter(s), Explore to build a Look with the dimension or measure that contains this HTML parameter, and a dashboard to add the Look into it and see how these parameters work in dashboards. We'll start with the LookML project. If you're on the Looker home page, find the **Develop** tab (usually in the menu on your left), click on it, and then click on **Projects**. On the LookML projects page, find your **lb_thelook_ecommerce** project and click on it.

How to do it...

To add the HTML parameter to your dimension or measure, do the following:

1. Go to your LookML project and open the `orders view`.
2. Find the status dimension, then after the SQL line add the HTML code. Your dimension will look like this (the `{%` symbol is used to initiate Liquid tags within your LookML code):

```
dimension: status {
  type: string
  sql: ${TABLE}.status ;;
  html: {% if value == 'Complete' %}
  <p
    style="color: black; background-color: lightblue;
    font-size: 100%; text-align:center">{{ rendered_value }}</p>
```

```
{% elsif value == 'Shipped' %}
<p
  style="color: black; background-color: lightgreen;
  font-size: 100%; text-align:center">{{ rendered_value }}</p>
{% else %}
<p
  style="color: black; background-color: orange;
  font-size: 100%; text-align:center">{{ rendered_value }}</p>
{% endif %}
;;
}
```

3. In the top-right corner, click on **Save Changes**.

4. Click on the arrow near `orders.view` above the code editor and choose **Explore Orders**.

5. In the Explore environment, choose **Order ID** and **Status**.

6. Add a filter by **Delivered Date**, then add **2022/09/01** as a filter.

7. Press **Run**.

8. Note the colors under the **Status** column (*Figure 5.4*).

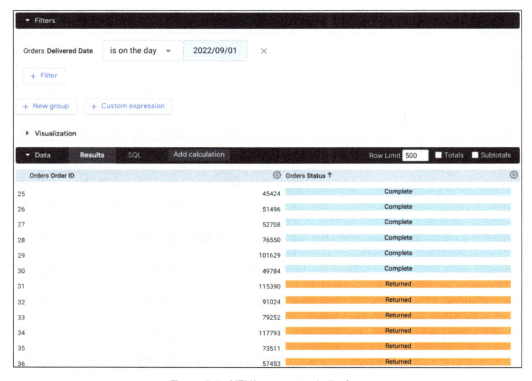

Figure 5.4 – HTML parameter in Explore

To add another HTML parameter to your dimension or measure, do the following:

1. Go to your LookML project and open Users view.

2. Find the country dimension, then after SQL line add the following HTML code (this will add a small planet icon to every country name):

```
html:<p><img src="https://upload.wikimedia.org/wikipedia/
commons/thumb/f/f3/Emblem-earth.svg/1024px-Emblem-earth.svg.png"
alt="" height="20" width="20">{{ rendered_value }}</p>;;
```

3. Click on **Save Changes**.

4. Click on the arrow near users.view above the code editor and choose **Explore Users**.

5. Choose **Country** and **Count**.

6. Press **Run** (*Figure 5.5*).

7. Choose **Column visualization**.

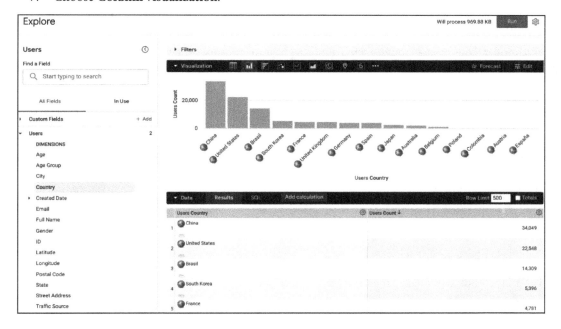

Figure 5.5 – HTML parameter in Explore

8. Click on the gear icon near the **Run** button and click on **Save | To an existing dashboard**. Choose **Ecommerce Dashboard**.

9. Go to the dashboard, move the tiles as you like.

See also

- More about the HTML parameter: `https://cloud.google.com/looker/docs/reference/param-field-html`

- Conditional formatting in LookML with the HTML parameter: `https://cloud.google.com/looker/docs/best-practices/cookbook-visualizations-conditional-formatting`

- *Getting the most out of Looker visualizations cookbook: Tooltip customization*: `https://cloud.google.com/looker/docs/best-practices/cookbook-visualizations-tooltip-customization`

Working with Liquid parameters in labels

Labels enhance the user experience of Explores by providing the option to customize the display of field names in the field picker and data table. We already explored `label` parameters earlier in this book. Now let's discuss how we can use Liquid variables in `label` parameters.

As a reminder, Looker uses Liquid, a templating language, to enhance content flexibility and dynamism. Within labels, Liquid allows you to dynamically change the label value based on various factors.

Getting ready

In this section, we will work in multiple environments: LookML to create the `label` parameter(s) and Explore to build a Look with the dimension or measure that contains this parameter. We'll start with the LookML project. If you're on the Looker home page, find the **Develop** tab (usually in the menu on your left), click on it, then click on **Projects**. On the LookML projects page, find your **lb_thelook_ecommerce** project and click on it.

How to do it...

To add the `label` parameter with Liquid to your dimension or measure, do the following:

1. In the LookML project, open the `orders view`.
2. Find the Count measure.
3. After the `type:count` line, add the following code:

```
label: "{{ _explore._name}}: Count"
```

4. Click **Save Changes**.
5. Click on the arrow near `orders.view` above the code editor and choose **Explore Orders**.
6. You will see that the Count measure will look like **orders: Count**. The label changes the measure name dynamically, appending the Explore name we are working on to the name of the measure.

7. Click on the "burger" (or three-lines) menu button in Explore and search for **Orders and Users** Explore. The name of the Count measure will be different for this Explore – it changes dynamically (*Figure 5.6*).

8. Choose any dimension and Count measure and press **Run**.

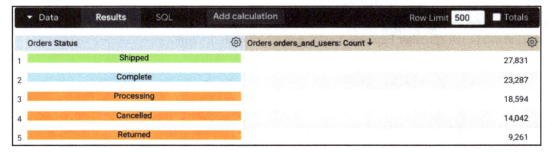

Figure 5.6 – Dynamic label parameter in Explore

In the preceding screenshot (*Figure 5.6*), you can see our Count measure changed to display the Explore's name: `orders_and_users: Count`.

There's more...

A popular way to make your labels dynamic is to use `user_attributes` – it allows for the labels/names of the fields to be changed depending on the person that analyses data:

```
dimension: name {
  label: "{% if _user_attributes['company'] == 'Looker' %}
    Employee Name {% else %} Customer Name {% endif %}"
  sql: ${TABLE}.name ;;
}
```

In Looker, user attributes are custom key-value pairs that can be associated with individual users or groups. These attributes provide a flexible way to store and manage additional information about users, which can then be used to personalize their experience in Looker. Looker user attributes are configured in the **Admin** section; we will explore them later in this book.

See also

- Labels for fields: `https://cloud.google.com/looker/docs/reference/param-field-label`

- Interesting ways to use Liquid in labels: `https://cloud.google.com/looker/docs/best-practices/how-to-use-liquid-in-labels`

- Liquid variable reference: `https://cloud.google.com/looker/docs/liquid-variable-reference`

Working with dynamic SQL

The SQL parameter supports a variety of SQL expressions that serve the purpose of defining dimensions, measures, and filters. We already explored it earlier in this book. Now, let's discuss how we can use Liquid variables in SQL parameters.

It is worth mentioning, in this chapter, the parameter element in Looker. It creates a filter-only field that can be used to filter Explores, Looks, and dashboards. It cannot be added to a result set:

```
view: view_name {
  parameter: parameter_name { ... }
}
```

We will use this parameter element in this recipe.

Getting ready

In this section, we will work in multiple environments: LookML to create the SQL parameter(s) and Explore to build a Look with the dimension or measure that contains this parameter. We'll start with the LookML project. If you're on the Looker home page, find the **Develop** tab (usually in the menu on your left), click on it, and then click on **Projects**. On the LookML projects page, find your **lb_thelook_ecommerce** project and click on it.

How to do it...

To add the sql parameter with Liquid elements to your dimension or measure, do the following:

1. Go to the orders view in your LookML project. As usual, click on it to open the view in the code editor.

2. At the end of the code file, just before the last }, add the following parameter code (the parameter parameter creates a field exclusively for filtering in Explores, Looks, and dashboards – it cannot be included in result sets):

```
parameter: break_down_by_date {
  type: unquoted
  allowed_value: {
    label: "Break down by Day"
    value: "day"
  }
  allowed_value: {
    label: "Break down by Month"
    value: "month"
  }
  allowed_value: {
    label: "Break down by Year"
```

```
      value: "year"
    }
  }
```

3. Below this `parameter` block of code, add the following dimension:

```
dimension: date {
  sql:
    {% if break_down_by_date._parameter_value == 'day' %}
      ${created_date}
    {% elsif break_down_by_date._parameter_value == 'month' %}
      ${created_month}
    {% elsif break_down_by_date._parameter_value == 'year' %}
      ${created_year}
    {% else %}
      ${created_date}
    {% endif %};;
}
```

4. Click **Save Changes**.

5. Click on the arrow near `orders.view` above the code editor and choose **Explore Orders**
    (*Figure 5.7*).

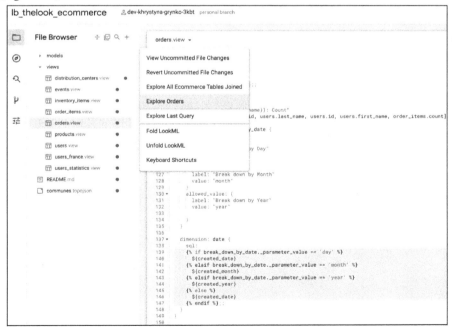

Figure 5.7 – Dynamic SQL parameter in LookML

6. In the `Orders` Explore, note the appearance of a new **FILTER-ONLY FIELDS** section, on the left side of the Explore interface, with the **Break Down by Date** field. Click on it – it will appear in the filters. Choose **Break Down By Year**.

7. On the left side of the Explore, choose the **Date** field (the one that we created previously with the Liquid `SQL` parameter), and the **Count** field (or `orders: Count`).

8. Press **Run**. Analyze the results (*Figure 5.8*).

Figure 5.8 – Dynamic SQL parameter in Explore

In the preceding exercise, using the dynamic `SQL` parameter, we simplified our Explore user experience.

There's more...

The dynamic `SQL` parameter can also be used with `user_attributes` like in labels, to customize what data is shown to Explore users and how it's presented. For example, in the following code, we hide the `salary` field (`hidden: yes`) but create a new one called `Salary Display` that will show salaries to the human resources department, and show the message `Salary Hidden` to others:

```
dimension: salary {
  type: number
  hidden: yes
  sql: ${TABLE}.user_id ;;
}

dimension: salary_display {
  sql:
    {% if _user_attributes['HR'] == 'yes' %}
      ${salary}
    {% else %}
```

```
        "Salary Hidden"
      {% endif %} ;;
  }
```

The `user_attributes` element will be explained later in this book.

See also

- SQL (for fields): `https://cloud.google.com/looker/docs/reference/param-field-sql#liquid_variables_with_sql`

- About parameter elements: `https://cloud.google.com/looker/docs/reference/param-field-parameter`

- Liquid in SQL statement for derived table: `https://www.googlecloudcommunity.com/gc/Modeling/Liquid-in-SQL-statement-for-derived-table/td-p/565469`

- Creating dynamic SQL derived tables with LookML and Liquid lab: `https://www.cloudskillsboost.google/catalog_lab/4090`

Working with actions

Actions in Looker can be a very powerful feature. It gives the possibility to users to connect from Looker to third-party tools to build data-driven workflows, to make the Looker environment interactive and the data actionable.

The `action` parameter in LookML gives users the possibility to perform field-level tasks directly from an Explore, Look, or dashboard.

The `action` parameter can be used to initiate external workflows or processes, such as sending emails, creating Jira tickets, or updating CRM records. This allows users to seamlessly integrate Looker with other tools and applications they use in their day-to-day work.

In this recipe, we will explain how to add an `action` parameter to LookML that will trigger a Zap in a Zapier application.

Zapier is an automation platform that connects different web applications and APIs to enable users to automate tasks between them. With Zapier, you can create "Zaps," which are workflows that automate tasks between multiple applications.

You will need to have a Zap configured in Zapier in order to follow along. You can start with Zapier for free. Links providing information on how to work with Zapier are available at the end of this recipe in the *See also* section.

If you don't have Zapier or any other similar application integrated with Looker and you don't want to set it up at this stage, you can just review the steps to understand how the `action` parameter works. Note that there are two types of actions in Looker: those from the Action Hub server and those defined within LookML with the actions parameter. We will review both in this recipe.

Getting ready

In this section, we will work in multiple environments: the **Admin** panel, a LookML project to create the `action` parameter(s), and Explore to build a Look with the dimension or measure that contains this parameter. We'll start with the LookML project. If you're on the Looker home page, find the **Develop** tab (usually in the menu on your left), click on it, and then click on **Projects**. On the LookML projects page, find your **lb_thelook_ecommerce** project and click on it.

How to do it...

Let's first explore the Looker Action Hub:

1. Click on the burger menu button in the top-left corner near the Looker logo.
2. Click on **Admin**.
3. In the **Admin** menu, find **Platforms** and then click on **Actions**.
4. From the Looker actions, you'll find a list of services integrated with Looker. To use these services as actions in Looker, they should be enabled – there is an **Enable** button for that.
5. If you don't find a service to connect your Looker with, you can scroll to the end of the Looker **Actions** page and find the button **Add Action Hub**. (This chapter won't explain how to create a new integration. A link on how to create your own Action Hub is provided at the end of the "Working with Actions" section, in See also section of this recipe.)
6. Click on the **Enable** button next to one of the services – for example, Airtable.
7. To be enabled, the AirTable action requires an API key that is available in your Airtable account (if you use Airtable): `https://www.basegenius.com/airpower/help/how-to-find-airtable-api-key/`.
8. Go back to the Looker actions, find Zapier, and enable it if you have a Zapier account (*Figure 5.9*).

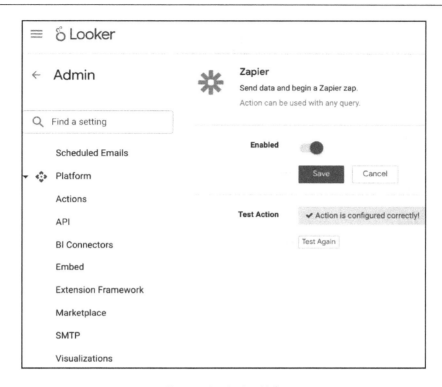

Figure 5.9 – Action Hub

9. By enabling an action in Looker, we connect it to a compatible app. This allows users within Explores to directly manipulate data, such as sending it to the connected app for further use (in the Explore, click on the gear icon in the top - right corner near Run button then click on Send - the enabled app will appear there).

Another way to use Actions in Looker, is to add the `action` parameter to your dimension or measure, let's do the following:

1. Go to the LookML project and open the `orders.view` in your code editor.

2. Scroll to the end of the file, and just before the last `}`, let's add the following code to create a new dimensions called "actions" (the `action` parameter can be added to any dimension, but in this case, we want to have a dedicated actions dimension). You can copy the full code from the GitHub repository in *Chapter 5*, (`https://github.com/PacktPublishing/Business-Intelligence-with-Looker-Cookbook/blob/main/Chapter05`):

```
dimension: actions {
  sql: "Actions..." ;;
  action: {
    label: "Email Data Quality Team"
```

```
url: "https://hooks.zapier.com/hooks/catch/(replace_by_your_
      code)/(replace_by_your_code)/"
      #add your webhook URL here
icon_url: "http://www.google.com/s2/favicons?domain=www.
      gmail.com"

form_param: {...
```

The full code is available in the GitHub repository of Chapter 5: `https://github.com/PacktPublishing/Business-Intelligence-with-Looker-Cookbook/blob/main/Chapter05`

> **Important note**
> Even if you don't have a Zapier webhook URL at this stage, it's okay; you can still try this code out. It won't send the real action to Zapier, but you will see what the `action` parameter looks like in your newly created Actions dimension in the Explore.

3.   Click on **Save Changes**.

4.   Click on the arrow near `orders.view` above the code editor and choose **Explore Orders**.

5.   In the `Orders` Explore, choose the **Order ID**, **Status**, and **Actions** fields.

6.   Add the **Status is Cancelled** filter.

7.   Press **Run**.

8.   In the **Results** section, click on the three dots near **Actions** in the **Actions** column.

Figure 5.10—Orders Explore

9. Click on **Email Data Quality Team** and the pre-filled form will appear. The form can be completed if needed and sent to the team (if we have the correct Zapier URL).

How it works...

Now let's analyze the elements of our `action` parameter one by one:

The `action` parameter can be added to any dimension or measure; it doesn't have to be a specific Actions dimension as in our case. A dimension or measure can have multiple `action` parameters if we want to provide multiple options (for example, `Text Security Consultant`, `Send Email to Data Team`, `Send the Data to Slack`, or `Create Jira Ticket`).

- `label` (as always) permits us to provide a clear and understandable name to our action.

- `url` is a string that specifies the URL to process the action (usually comes from an external app such as Zapier or Slack).

- `icon_url` is a visual element, an icon near your action's name.

- `form_param` specifies what should be in the form that will open before the action is sent to the third-party tool. You can add to the form elements of different types (`textarea`, `select`, or `string`), making them required or not, or with options or without.

There's more...

You can customize data actions to include user attributes (such as credentials) within the JSON payload. This allows for targeted operations against external services based on the individual user (`https://cloud.google.com/looker/docs/admin-panel-users-user-attributes#data_actions`).

Unlike data actions, which are defined within LookML, actions served through an Action Hub server are handled by a separate system. The Looker Action Hub lets you seamlessly connect Looker with popular services to streamline workflows. Data sent through actions is securely processed by the Action Hub for efficiency. You can find setup instructions in the actions documentation: `https://cloud.google.com/looker/docs/action-hub`.

See also

- Action field parameter: `https://cloud.google.com/looker/docs/reference/param-field-action`

- Sharing data through an Action Hub: `https://cloud.google.com/looker/docs/action-hub`

- Looker actions overview: `https://cloud.google.com/looker/docs/actions-overview`

- Looker Community – Actions: `https://www.googlecloudcommunity.com/gc/forums/searchpage/tab/message?advanced=false&allow_punctuation=false&filter=location&location=forum-board:looker-administering&q=actions`

- Trigger Zaps from webhooks `https://help.zapier.com/hc/en-us/articles/8496288690317-Trigger-Zaps-from-webhooks`

6
Troubleshooting Looker

Looker, a powerful data analytics platform, can sometimes present challenges that hinder its seamless operation. This chapter delves into the nuances of troubleshooting Looker, providing valuable insights and techniques to effectively resolve common issues. Equipped with this comprehensive guide, you can confidently navigate the Looker environment, ensuring a smooth and productive data analytics experience. From untangling error messages to fine-tuning query performance, this chapter will empower you to tackle any obstacle with finesse and extract actionable insights from data.

In this chapter, we're going to cover the following recipes:

- Troubleshooting LookML errors
- Exploring Content Validator
- Troubleshooting SQL through SQL runner
- Data tests
- Other ways to solve common Looker problems

Technical requirements

There are no specific requirements or preparation steps for this chapter. We will continue working with our **thelook_ecommerce** dataset (`https://console.cloud.google.com/marketplace/product/bigquery-public-data/thelook-ecommerce`), switching regularly between LookML, Explore, and dashboard environments inside Looker. We won't be working with BigQuery (which is the data warehouse used in this book) as we assume our dataset is already connected to Looker and ready to be used in it. But you can keep the **BigQuery** tab open to preview the tables and get familiarized with the data you'll be exploring in Looker.

Troubleshooting LookML errors

The LookML Validator serves as a comprehensive tool for LookML code validation, meticulously scrutinizing the syntax of object definitions (dimensions, measures, etc.) and established relationships (joins). It examines the entire LookML code within a model, ensuring that all elements adhere to the expected structure and formatting. The LookML Validator's scope does not extend to verifying SQL parameters associated with LookML objects (such as SQL derived tables). However, it does validate the $ { } fields within the SQL parameter.

Getting ready

In this section, we will work in the LookML project. To go to your LookML project if you're on the Looker home page, find the **Develop** tab (usually in the menu on the left), click on it, then click on **Projects**. On the LookML projects page, find your **lb_thelook_ecommerce** project and click on it. Open one of the views in the LookML code editor – for example, **events.view**.

How to do it...

To create and then troubleshoot a LookML error, let's do the following:

1. In events.view, find any dimension, for example id.

2. After the SQL line, click **Enter** and add any letter, for example a.

3. On your right, in the **Quick Help** section, you will see the immediate error detections and an explanation of what exactly is wrong (*Figure 6.1*):

    Expecting 'end_of_file', 'keyword', '{', '}', ']', 'comma', ':', got 'identifier'

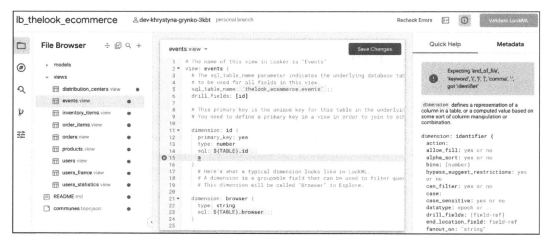

Figure 6.1 – Immediate error detection in LookML

If you don't see the **Quick Help** section on your page, click on the **i** icon in the top - right corner.

Let's create another LookML error to see the immediate error detection:

1. Replace a from the previous example with `hidden: maybe`.

2. In the **Quick Help** section on your right, you will immediately see the message: **Must provide "yes" or "no" for "hidden".**

There is a magic button, **Validate LookML**, that you can click to verify LookML errors when Looker doesn't see them immediately. LookML validation is a necessary step before pushing your changes into production. Remember, the LookML Validator cannot debug SQL errors. It does not validate the raw SQL code after the SQL parameter. Any SQL errors will be reported during runtime when Looker sends the statement to your database for execution.

Let's test the LookML Validator in action:

1. Go to `users.view` and add the following code after any dimension:

    ```
    dimension: location {
      type: location
      sql: ${TABLE}.users_location ;;
    }
    ```

2. Click on **Save Changes**.

3. Then click on **Validate LookML**.

4. The **Project Health** section will open to replace **Quick Help**.

5. In **Project Health**, check the LookML validation part. You will see the following warning there:

    The "location" field type requires both "sql_latitude" and "sql_longitude".

    Learn more.

    users.view:122 lb_thelook_ecommerce:orders

6. The warning message explains that if you use a `location-type` dimension, you need two additional parameters to be included. If this explanation is not clear enough, you can click on **Learn More**.

7. The `users.view:122 lb_thelook_ecommerce:orders` part is clickable as well. It brings you to the place where the error sits (the number of the line where my error sits is 122; your number might be different).

8. Now delete the location dimension that creates warnings.

9. Click on **Save Changes**.

10. Then click on **Validate LookML**.

11. In the top-right corner, click on **Commit Changes & Push** to save everything to your Git environment.

12. Click **Deploy to Production**. Now you can see **Up To Date** in the top-right corner.

Now let's see a real LookML error (and not a warning) in LookML validation:

1. In one of the previous chapters, we created `users_statistics.view` and referenced it in our model.

2. Let's delete this view by clicking on the three dots near the view name in the **File Browser** section of the page.

3. Click on **Validate LookML**.

4. In LookML errors in the **Project Health** section, you might see the following:

```
There are serious errors with this LookML code that could
prevent queries from running.
Unknown view "users_statistics".
Learn more.
lb_thelook_ecommerce.model:29 lb_thelook_ecommerce:users_
statistics


Explore name must match a view name, or the explore must provide
a 'from:' or 'view_name:' property
lb_thelook_ecommerce.model:29


Explore name must match a view name, or the explore must provide
a 'from:' or 'view_name:' property
models/lb_thelook_ecommerce:29
```

The preceding errors show you the problems related to your `users_statistics.view` deletion. Because this view is referenced in multiple places, LookML Validator shows you that you cannot move further unless you delete the mentions of the deleted `users_statistics.view` (*Figure 6.2*).

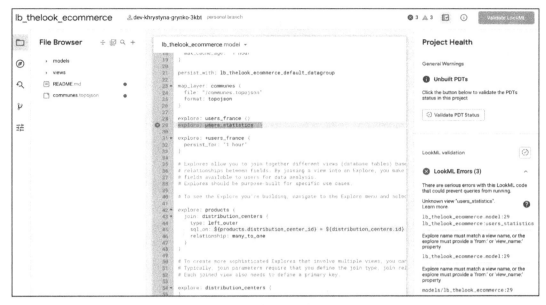

Figure 6.2 – LookML validation errors

5. Delete `users_statistics.view` from your model.

6. Click on **Save Changes**.

7. Click on **Validate LookML** – you'll see the **No LookML errors found** message in **Project Health**.

8. To restore the deleted view or cancel any changes, in **Git Actions**, you can click on **Revert to...** and go back to the version that was deployed to production (*Figure 6.3*).

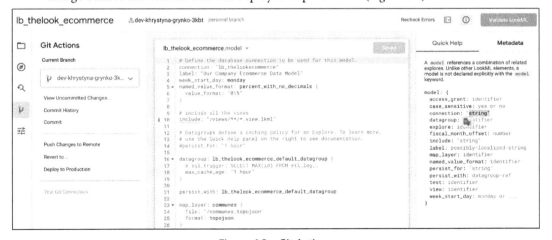

Figure 6.3 – Git Actions

Looker leverages Git to track changes and maintain file versions. Each LookML project is associated with a Git repository, and each developer branch mirrors a Git branch. Looker can seamlessly integrate with various Git providers, including GitHub, GitLab, and Bitbucket.

See also

- Looker error catalog: `https://cloud.google.com/looker/docs/error-catalog`
- Using version control and deploying: `https://cloud.google.com/looker/docs/version-control-and-deploying-changes`
- LookML reference overview: `https://cloud.google.com/looker/docs/reference/lookml-quick-reference`
- Google Cloud Community – Looker Modeling: `https://www.googlecloudcommunity.com/gc/forums/filteredbylabelpage/board-id/looker-modeling/label-name/lookml`

Exploring the Content Validator

The Content Validator meticulously scans your LookML code to identify references to models, Explores, and field names that are embedded within your Looker content. It serves as a valuable tool for verifying the integrity of LookML references, rectifying errors introduced by LookML modifications, and updating the names of LookML elements throughout your project. To access the Content Validator, you need the **developer** permission.

Getting ready

To launch the Content Validator, select **Content Validator** from the **Develop** menu in the left-hand navigation pane.

How to do it...

The Content Validator can be utilized in two distinct ways:

1. **Validate**: To identify and resolve errors stemming from changes made to your LookML model.
2. **Find & Replace in All Content**: To locate and replace models, Explores, or field names across your Looker content, regardless of whether errors exist in the Looker content.

When in the Content Validator interface, do the following:

1. Click **Validate** and wait for Looker to check for errors. If no errors are found, do the following:

   I. Go back to your LookML project (in the left panel in Content Validator, you have the search bar to find your **lb_thelook_ecommerce** project).

   II. Go to users.view and rename one of the dimensions or measures that are used in your dashboard, for example, the one we created in one of the previous chapters: Ecommerce Dashboard.

   III. In this dashboard, we used the age_group dimension. Let's rename it to something else.

   IV. Click **Save Changes** and **Validate LookML**: you will see a message **No LookML errors found** in LookML validation section of the Project Health panel in the right part of a screen.

2. Go back to the Content Validator (**Menu -> Develop -> Content Validator** and then click on **Validate** to check the content again (*Figure 6.4*).

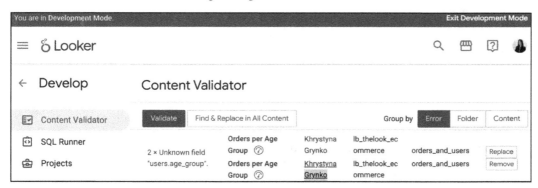

Figure 6.4 – Content Validator

3. If you have multiple errors, you can group the results of this validation by **Error** (type of error), by **Folder**, and by **Content**.

4. In our example (*Figure 6.4*), the Content Validator shows that our **Orders per Age Group** dashboard element (tile) contains the unknown field users.age_group – we renamed it previously so our Look (tile) doesn't recognize it anymore.

5. You can click **Replace** to replace the field with the new/renamed field.

6. Or, you can remove the field from the content (*Figure 6.5*).

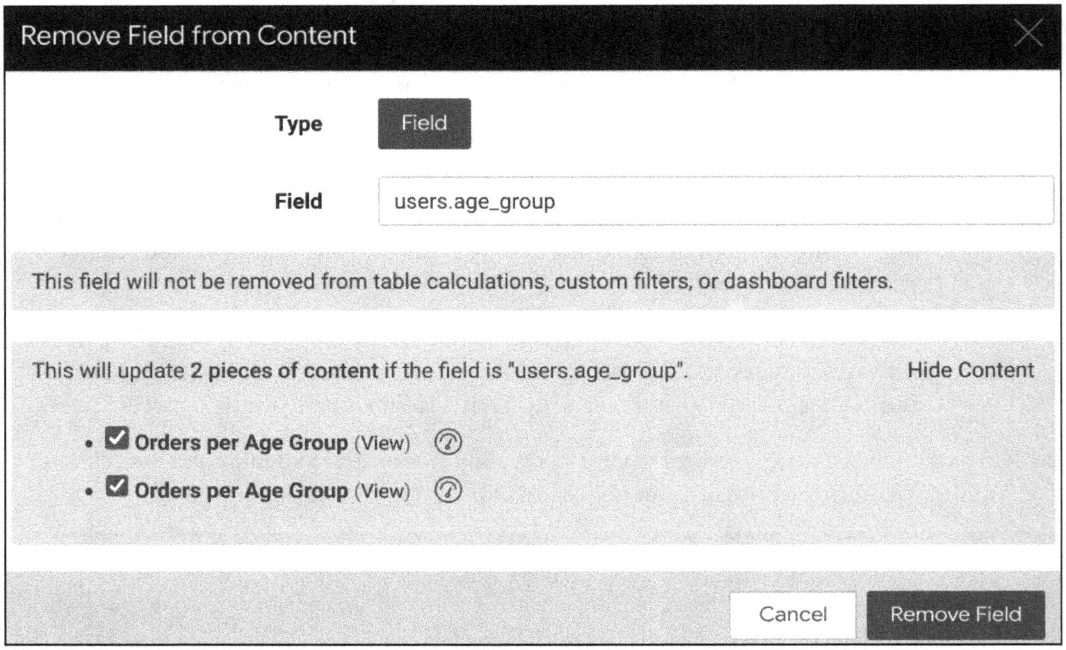

Figure 6.5 – Remove Field

> **Important note**
> The Content Validator lacks an undo feature and has the potential to impact a significant number of Looks, dashboards, and their associated **Explore from Here** links. If an error occurs, strive to rectify it promptly to prevent additional changes from complicating the identification of affected Looks.

How it works...

The Content Validator helps you find and fix errors caused by changes to your LookML code. For example, if you rename a field from "customer" to "user," any Looks or dashboard tiles that used the "customer" field will stop working (unless you used the "alias" parameter). The Content Validator will show you all the places where the "customer" field is used and give you an easy way to fix the error. Upon running the Content Validator, it scrutinizes all references within your Looks and dashboards to your LookML models, Explores, views, and fields. It subsequently generates an error message for any references your content makes to an unidentified LookML object.

The Content Validator does not display errors for the following scenarios:

- Content for which you lack the requisite **developer** permission
- Looks that have been deleted and are in the **Trash** folder

See also

- Content validation: `https://cloud.google.com/looker/docs/content-validation`

Troubleshooting SQL through SQL Runner

SQL Runner is a way to debug your SQL-based Looker issues that cannot be verified by LookML and the Content Validator.

SQL Runner in Looker grants direct access to your database or data warehouse connected to Looker, enabling a range of data exploration and management capabilities. With SQL Runner, you can browse schema tables, construct Explores from SQL queries, execute predefined descriptive queries, access SQL Runner history, download query results, share queries, incorporate them into LookML projects as derived tables, and perform various other useful tasks.

Getting ready

In this section, we will mostly use LookML, Explore, and SQL Runner interfaces. You can open **Users Explore** in one tab and have the LookML project open in another browser tab.

How to do it...

As a debugging tool, SQL Runner can be accessed in two ways and usually for two principal reasons:

1. In Explore, if you obtain a result that does not seem correct to you and you want to understand the query behind the result, then follow the next few steps:

    I.   Open any Explore of your **lb_thelook_ecommerce** model – for example, **users**.

    II. Click on the **Age Group** and **# of Users** (or the **Count** measure) fields.

    III. Click **Run** to get the columns with data in the **Results** tab.

    IV. Click on the **SQL** section near the **Results** tab.

    V.   Click on **Open** in SQL Runner (*Figure 6.6*).

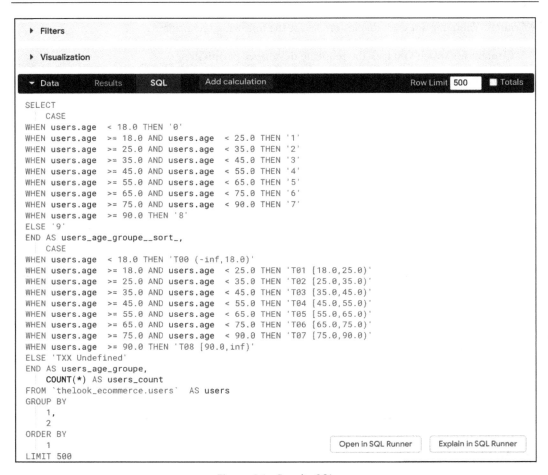

Figure 6.6 – Results SQL

VI.   On the SQL Runner page, you can debug your SQL query, make any changes, click **Run** to see the results, and even visualize the data (*Figure 6.7*).

Figure 6.7 – SQL Runner

2. In *Chapter 2*, we created a Users France view based on the derived table built with SQL (check *Figure 6.8*).

Figure 6.8 – View based on derived table

I.   If you don't have this view, click on + near **File Browser** in your LookML project interface,
       click on **Create View**, and start the view with the following code:

```
view: users_france {
  derived_table: {
    sql:
    SELECT *
    FROM users
    WHERE country = "France"
    ;;
  }
}
```

II.   Dimensions and measures that go after this code can be copied from users.view.

III.   When you've created users_france.view, or if you found the one we created
       previously, let's add a small error to our SQL code that creates this view – delete the "
       after France:

```
WHERE country = "France
```

IV.   In the top-right corner of the LookML editor, click on **Save Changes**.

V.   Then click on **Validate LookML: No errors found**. The LookML Validator doesn't check the SQL errors.

VI.   Above the code editor, let's click on the arrow near `users_france.view` and choose **Explore Users France** to be redirected to the **Explore** page.

VII.   On the Explore page, click on any field (**Age Group**, for example) and click **Run**.

VIII.   There will be no results and Looker will display an error message (*Figure 6.9*).

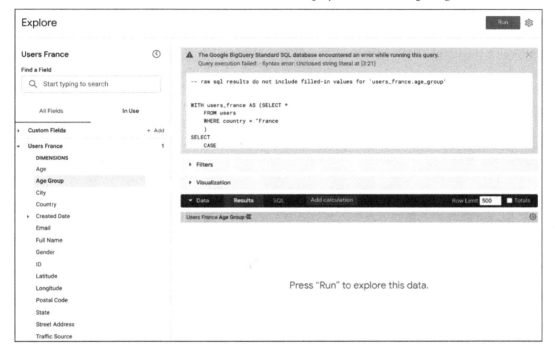

Figure 6.9 – Explore SQL error

IX.   In the **SQL** tab, near **Results**, copy the underlying query.

X.   If the **Open in SQL Runner** button is not available, open the Looker menu on your left, find **Develop**, then **SQL Runner**.

XI.   In SQL Runner, in **Connection**, choose the db/dwh connection your LookML project is based on, choose **LookML project**, and paste the copied SQL query.

XII.   Correct the error in the query and click **Run** to check if it works after the correction.

XIII.   After the debugging in the SQL query, go back to LookML to make the necessary changes in your code (by clicking on the **Menu** button in the top-left corner, then **Develop**, then choose your LookML project).

When clicking on the gear icon in the top-right corner of the SQL Runner interface, you can do the following:

- Download the SQL query
- Add it to the project (as a derived view)
- Get the LookML code for the derived table
- Click on **Explore** to go back to the Explore

There's more...

There is an **Explain in SQL Runner** button available in the **SQL** tab in **Explore**. When you click that button, the query is loaded into SQL Runner inside an EXPLAIN function. It is used to understand how the query is executed by the database, for example, to look for table scans, missing partitions, or other potential performance bottlenecks. The EXPLAIN function is not available for all database and data warehouses dialects.

Read more on this function here: `https://www.googlecloudcommunity.com/gc/Technical-Tips-Tricks/How-to-Optimize-SQL-with-EXPLAIN/ta-p/587526`

See also

- SQL Runner basics: `https://cloud.google.com/looker/docs/sql-runner-basics`
- Common SQL error troubleshooting tips in Looker: `https://www.googlecloudcommunity.com/gc/Technical-Tips-Tricks/Common-SQL-error-troubleshooting-tips-in-Looker/ta-p/586852`
- Troubleshooting Data Models in Looker – Lab: `https://www.cloudskillsboost.google/focuses/33371?parent=catalog`

Data tests

Looker provides a couple of tools to ensure the accuracy and integrity of your data models and visualizations:

- The LookML Validator checks for syntactic errors in your LookML code
- The Content Validator verifies that object references within your content align with your data model

Data tests (the test parameter) enable you to validate the logic of your model, to perform unit testing before pushing new code into production, by creating queries and corresponding yes/no assertion statements. The data test executes the test query and verifies that the assertion holds true for each row of the query. If the assertion evaluates yes for every row, the data test is considered successful.

The test parameter has the following subparameters:

- `explore_source`: Defines the query that provides the data for your test
- `assert`: Sets the criteria your data must meet to pass the test

If your project settings mandate that data tests pass before deployment to production, and if your project contains at least one test parameter, the **Integrated Development Environment** (IDE) or LookML editor will present the **Run Tests** button upon committing changes.

Getting ready

We'll be working in the LookML environment. To access it, open the Looker menu, then **Develop**, then **Projects**, and find your **lb_thelook_ecommerce** project.

How to do it...

To add a data test in your project, let's do the following:

1. In the LookML project, click on + near **File Browser**, and choose **Create Generic LookML File**. Name it `data_tests`.

2. Add the following code in this new file:

```
test: order_id_is_unique {
  explore_source: orders {
    column: order_id {}
    column: count {}
    sorts: [orders.count: desc]
    limit: 1
  }
  assert: order_id_is_unique {
    expression: ${orders.count} = 1 ;;
  }
}
```

3. Click on **Save Changes**. The idea of this test code is to verify whether the user ID used in our project contains the unique value (we want every user to have a unique ID).

4. Data test code can be added to view and model files. If you added it separately in the generic file like we did in this section, don't forget to include this test in your model with the following line of code:

```
include: "/data_tests.lkml"
```

5. Click on **Save Changes**.

6. If you don't know the URL path of your file, you can always click on the three dots near the view, model, or any other file, then click on **Copy File Path**.

7. Once the data test is added and the changes are saved, you can click on **Run Data Tests** in the **Project Health** section on the right (**Project Health** panel can be opened by clicking on the **Project Health** icon in the top-right corner, near **Validate LookML** and the **I** (**Quick Help** icon) (*Figure 6.10*).

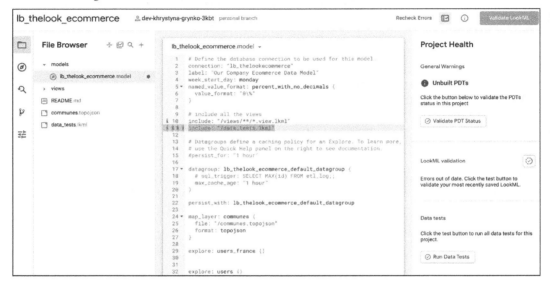

Figure 6.10 – Run data tests

If there is no error, you will see something such as **1 of 1 tests passed**.

There's more...

You can configure your project settings to require data tests to pass before deploying your files to production. With this, the IDE (LookML **Code Editor**) will present the **Run Tests** button after you commit changes to the project.

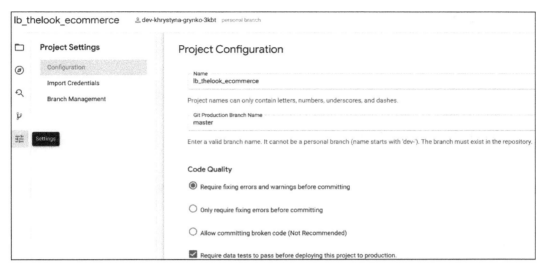

Figure 6.11 – Project configuration

You must be in **Development Mode** to run data tests.

See also

- Test parameter: `https://cloud.google.com/looker/docs/reference/param-model-test`

- LookML Data Tests: Recommendations and Best Practices: `https://www.googlecloudcommunity.com/gc/Modeling/LookML-Data-Tests-Recommendations-and-Best-Practices/m-p/568932`

Other ways to solve common Looker problems

Looker, a powerful data exploration and visualization tool, occasionally presents challenges that can hinder your data exploration journey. This section provides a way to navigate these challenges, ensuring you remain productive in your data analysis endeavors.

How to do it...

Let's review different ways to solve your Looker problems:

1. Try the Looker documentation at `https://cloud.google.com/looker/docs` and the free Looker training at `https://www.cloudskillsboost.google/paths/28` to review ways of doing what you're trying to achieve.

2. From the Looker (Google Cloud core) documentation, click **Send feedback** near the top - right of the page. This action will open a feedback form. Your comments will be reviewed by the Looker (Google Cloud core) team.

3. You can search your problem on the Looker Community forum at `https://www.googlecloudcommunity.com/gc/Looker/ct-p/looker`, and if you don't find a satisfying answer, you can post your question there as well.

4. You can leverage Cloud Logging capabilities to view and query logs for your Looker (Google Cloud core) instance: `https://cloud.google.com/looker/docs/looker-core-logging`

5. Use Cloud Audit Logs to help you answer the question *"Who did what, where, and when?"*: `https://cloud.google.com/looker/docs/looker-core-audit-logging`

6. You can also leverage Google Cloud paid support for your Looker problems. Find more information about Standard, Enhanced, and Premium support offers here: `https://cloud.google.com/support`

See also

- About Looker Support: `https://cloud.google.com/looker/docs/best-practices/about-looker-support`

7
Integrating Looker with Other Applications

Looker's ability to connect with third-party applications unlocks a powerful ecosystem for data-driven workflows. By connecting third-party tools to Looker, you create a single, governed data model. This ensures consistency in analysis and metrics across your entire organization, regardless of which BI tool people use.

Looker Actions, which we covered earlier in this book, transforms static dashboards into interactive ones, empowering users to execute meaningful tasks directly within the Looker interface, such as generating Jira tickets for the security team, dispatching data-driven reports via email to your data analysts, or sharing visualizations with colleagues through Slack, all without ever leaving Looker.

Third-party applications can leverage Looker's power through seamless connection. This means you can seamlessly pull fresh, Looker-modeled data directly into your preferred tools, eliminating the need for manual data transfers or context switching. Looker offers diverse integration options, including APIs and embedded dashboards. But this chapter dives specifically into the ready-made connectors embedded within third-party applications, showcasing how they streamline data access and workflow automation.

In this chapter, we're going to cover the following topics related to Looker's connection to external applications:

- Accessing Looker from Google Sheets
- Accessing Looker from Looker Studio
- Exploring other third-party integrations

Important note

Not all LookML features will work flawlessly through third-party connectors. Complex features such as Liquid variables might not be fully supported. It's essential to test compatibility carefully.

Accessing Looker from Google Sheets

Google Sheets is an online spreadsheet tool for organizing, analyzing, and sharing data, like a powerful online version of a paper spreadsheet. While modern BI tools offer robust features, some users simply prefer the familiar and accessible format of spreadsheets for data exploration. To maximize the efficiency and accuracy of user analysis within Google Sheets, we recommend connecting to Looker's modeled data sets. This eliminates the need for manual data preparation, ensuring users work with high-quality, readily analyzable information.

Getting ready

Using the Google account you used for Google Cloud Platform, go to Google Drive (`https://drive.google.com/`). In this section, we will create a new Google Sheet report in your Google Drive and connect it to Looker.

How to do it...

1. When in Google Drive, click on **New** in the top - left corner, then click on **Google Sheets** (*Figure 7.1*).

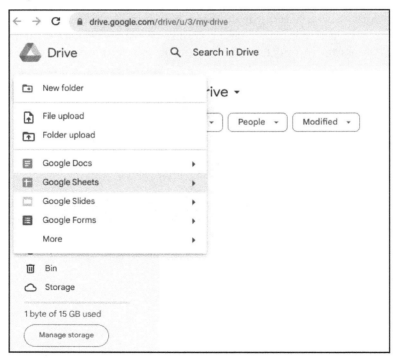

Figure 7.1 – Google Sheets in Google Drive

2. In your newly created spreadsheet, click on **Data** in the menu bar, then click on **Data connectors**, then click on **Connect to Looker** (*Figure 7.2*).

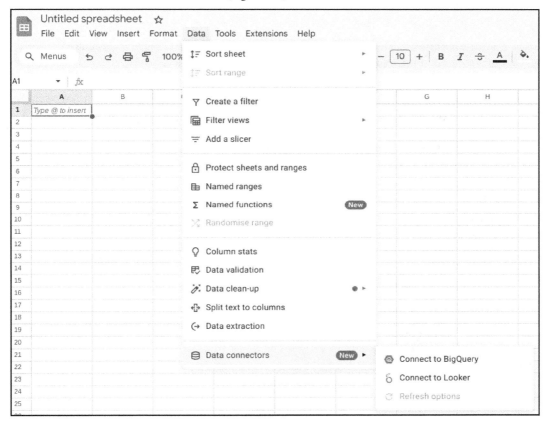

Figure 7.2 – Connect to Looker

3. In the **Connect to Looker** window, enter your Looker instance URL (you can find it in Google Cloud Platform when going to the Looker service page `https://console.cloud.google.com/looker/instances`) and click **Continue**.

4. Search for a model or choose the `lb_thelook_ecommerce` model from the list; click on it.

5. Search for `Orders` Explore and click **Connect**.

6. When you get the **Successfully connected to Looker** message, click on **Get Started**.

7. Now you can see your Explore's schema, and you can do the following with the data:

    - **Refresh options**: Refresh data if you are not sure it is up to date (if you created your connection some time ago).

    - **Schedule refresh**: Schedule a periodic refresh of the data so Google Sheets automatically refreshes the connection for you.

    - **Create pivot tables**: Pivot tables are powerful tools within Google Sheets that enable you to summarize, reorganize, and analyze large datasets interactively. In our case, it is the only way to work with our LookML-prepared data through Google Sheets.

8. Click the **Pivot table** button in the toolbar. Choose **New sheet** and click on **Create**. You can still use the **orders** tab to check the schema if you have forgotten what data was in your Orders Explore (note that your Orders Explore is based on the join of two tables, Orders and Users; it might be a good idea to rename the Explore in the LookML to make that clearer to data users).

9. On the **Pivot Table** tab (note that you can rename tabs and the spreadsheet as you want), on the right-hand side of the page in the **Pivot table editor**, choose the following elements (*Figure 7.3*):

    - **Country** as **Rows**

    - **Created Month** as **Columns**

    - **Orders Count** as **Values**

    - **Created Year, greater than 2022** as **Filter**

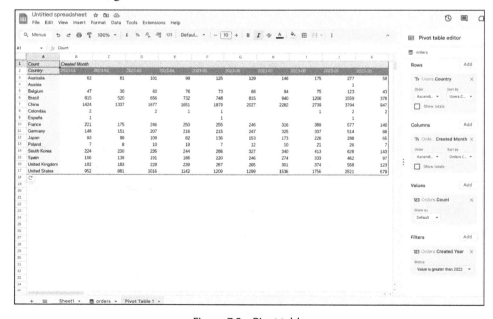

Figure 7.3 – Pivot table

10. After choosing these values in the editor, click on **Apply** under your pivot table so that Google Sheets can populate the data.

11. To build visualization highlight the table with data and click on **Insert -> Chart** in the toolbar.

12. To modify the visualization, you can change settings in the **Chart editor**; for example, do the following (*Figure 7.4*):

    I.   Choose **Line chart** as **Chart type**.

    II.   Tick the **Switch rows/columns** checkbox.

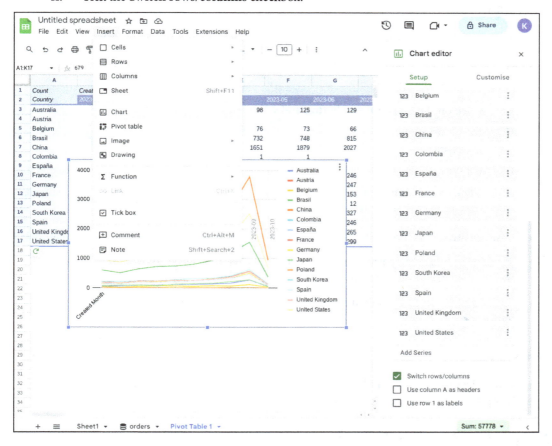

Figure 7.4 – Adding Chart in Connected Sheet

In the visualization, you now have the evolution of orders per country in 2023.

How it works...

Note that in some cases, the BI connection is not available by default. To enable it, your Looker administrator must enable either the **Looker BI Connectors** or the **Connected Sheets** toggle within the **BI Connectors** panel, found in the **Platform** section in the Admin menu in Looker interface.

Users must ensure their Looker login email matches their Google Workspace email. Otherwise, they'll encounter connection errors.

There's more...

Here's some useful information about Connected Sheets (Google Sheets and Looker):

- Looker admins can monitor Connected Sheets usage within the System Activity History Explore. For this do the following:

    I.   Click on the Looker menu button and select **Explore**.

    II.   In the search bar, type `System Activity` and select the **History** option within the results.

    III. On the Explore page, scroll through the **All Fields** section until you see **History** - click on it.

    IV.   Click on the dimension group titled **Query API Client Properties** to see fields available for Connected Sheet usage analysis.

- Case sensitivity in Google Sheets depends on the case sensitivity settings set up in the model

- Sheets users must have permission to Explore in Looker and be able to access the Looker model and the underlying database (in case of OAuth connection)

- Connected Sheets has certain data limits and might return errors in some cases (when queries return too much data)

See also

- Check Using Connected Sheets for Looker documentation page for more information: `https://cloud.google.com/looker/docs/connected-sheets`.

Accessing Looker from Looker Studio

Looker Studio (formerly Google Data Studio) is a web-based tool for building interactive dashboards and reports from diverse data sources such as BigQuery, Google Analytics, CSV files, and others. Looker Studio can connect to your Looker semantic layer (LookML model), letting you build dashboards and reports using your Looker's modeled data.

Additional integration between Looker and Looker Studio is planned for later.

Getting ready

Using the Google account you used for Google Cloud Platform, go to the Looker Studio website https://lookerstudio.google.com/. In this section, we will create a new Looker Studio report and connect it to Looker as a data source. Remember, Looker doesn't store data itself but instead uses a modeling layer to organize and prepare data from underlying databases or data warehouses for analysis.

How to do it...

1. On the Looker Studio website https://lookerstudio.google.com/, in the top - left corner under the logo, click on **Create** -> **Report**.

2. Once you click **Report**, Looker Studio prompts you to add data upon launching a new report, ensuring you start with the essential building blocks for your analysis. Click on Looker as a data source (*Figure 7.5*).

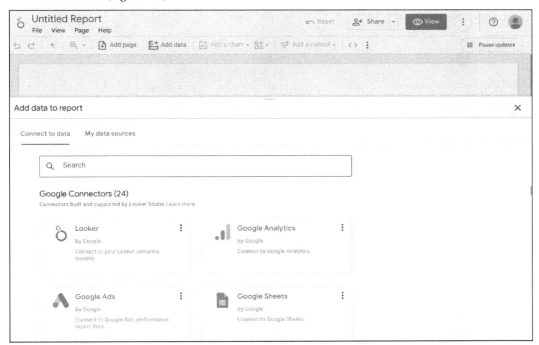

Figure 7.5 – Looker Studio

3. Authorize access to data, then enter your Looker instance URL and click on **Connect Looker account**.

4.   After connecting to your instance, choose the `Lb Thelook Ecommerce` model, then choose **Orders Explore** and click on **Add** in the bottom right corner.

5.   Now Looker Studio adds the first visualization to your report. Let's modify it in the right-hand section of the page. In **Dimension**, choose **Users Country**; in **Metric**, choose **Orders Count**. Click on **Chart** and change the chart type to **Bar** (*Figure 7.6*).

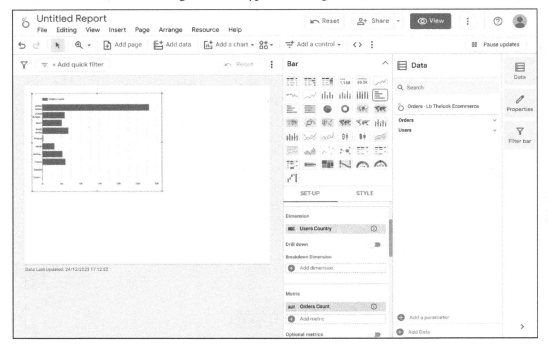

Figure 7.6 – Looker Studio

6.   You can make other modifications in your **SET-UP** and **STYLE** tabs on the right-hand side of the Looker Studio page. For example, if you scroll through the **SET-UP** section, you have the option to add a filter. In the filter, choose **Orders Created Year greater than 31/12/2022** to get the data for the period after (the year 2023 in our case).

7.   You can add other visualizations to your dashboard that will be based on the same Looker data source. To do this, you need to click **Add a chart** in the toolbar, choose a chart type, and make sure that the data source on the **SET-UP** tab is **Orders – Lb Thelook Ecommerce**.

You can add other visualizations to your dashboard with different data sources. You can also add text, lines, images, filters, and buttons to your Looker Studio dashboard to finalize it.

How it works...

In order to connect Looker Studio to Looker, you must have the Looker Studio connector enabled in the **Admin Platform** panel in Looker (in the latest version of Looker it is enabled by default).

To connect Looker Explore to Looker Studio, you must have explore permissions for at least one model within the Looker instance. If you only need to view existing Looker Studio reports based on Looker data, then the "viewer" permission level is sufficient.

There's more...

Looker admins can monitor Looker Studio usage within the System Activity History Explore (using the Query API Client Properties group of fields):

1. Click on the Looker menu button and select **Explore**.

2. In the search bar, type `System Activity` and select the **History** option within the results.

3. On the Explore page, scroll through the **All Fields** section until you see **History** -- click on it.

4. Click on the dimension group titled `Query API Client Properties` to see fields available for Looker Studio usage analysis.

See also

- Connecting to Looker Studio: `https://cloud.google.com/looker/docs/looker-studio-connector`.

Exploring other third-party integrations

Looker can connect to a vast array of third-party tools through its Action Hub. Additionally, a growing number of third-party tools are now able to connect to Looker directly from their interface. Admins can install the required Looker connector and configure authentication between Looker and **Tableau**, **Power BI**, and others. This section dives into how Looker connects with third-party tools, exploring the process and guiding you through the typical steps involved.

At the time of writing, Looker announced a new feature: Open SQL Interface. With this new feature, users can now connect to a LookML model as if it were a database. This allows them to take advantage of the work done by data analysts in LookML using the third-party tools they are most comfortable with. This enables you to access these LookML models from any third-party application that supports **Java Database Connectivity (JDBC)**.

Getting ready

Due to the vast number of third-party tools that can connect to Looker, this section will focus on the general steps applicable to many of them. While specific instructions won't be provided here, following these generic steps will equip you with a solid understanding of the connection process. By the end of this section, you'll find useful links to detailed documentation for connecting specific tools to Looker.

How to do it...

Once the Looker connector is installed and configured, you will be able to connect to Looker using the following steps (for more information on how to configure this connector, see the *See also* section):

1. Open the third-party tool interface.
2. Navigate to the settings or integrations section of the tool.
3. Look for an option to connect to Looker.
4. Click the option to connect to Looker.
5. Enter your Looker instance URL.
6. Click the button to connect. The third-party tool might open a browser window to connect to your Looker instance and authenticate your account with Oauth.
7. Once the connection is successful, you will be able to access Looker data from the third-party tool.

How it works...

Depending on the tool, additional steps might be added to the ones listed previously, such as when setting up the Looker–Tableau Connector. This involves adding the Tableau OAuth app to your Looker instance. The most convenient way to do this is through Looker's API Explorer, which simplifies the registration process. We will explore the API Explorer in the next chapter.

Tableau and other third-party connectors that support JDBC use the Open SQL Interface to connect to Looker. The OpenSQL Interface unlocks LookML models for any JDBC-supporting app, treating them like databases, and helps to leverage data analysts' work in your preferred tools (for example, by connecting your BI tool to a Looker modeling layer). More information about the Open SQL interface is available here: `https://cloud.google.com/looker/docs/sql-interface`.

There's more...

In addition to connecting to a Looker model from the third-party analysis tool, you can also send information or execute actions in third-party tools directly from Looker (for example, send Jira tickets, stop Google Ads campaigns, or send the data to Slack). To do that, you'll need Looker Actions. If a pre-built connection exists between Looker and your chosen tool, enable it within Action Hub in Looker Admin. If not, explore creating a custom connection using Actions Hub's setup. More information about Looker Actions is available here: `https://cloud.google.com/looker/docs/actions-overview`.

See also

- Tableau Connector:

  `https://cloud.google.com/looker/docs/tableau-connector`

- Power BI Connector:

  `https://cloud.google.com/looker/docs/powerbi-connector`

  `https://cloud.google.com/looker/docs/powerbi-service-connector`

- Sending Looker content to Slack:

  `https://cloud.google.com/looker/docs/best-practices/how-to-use-the-looker-slack-attachment-api-token-action`

8
Organizing the Looker Environment

While managing a handful of dashboards and Looks in Looker is straightforward, the platform is not intended to handle just a few visualizations. As a Looker user, especially with admin access, you may eventually face the challenge of managing a vast amount of content created by different users. Looker offers several organization options to address this complexity, including folders, favorites, and boards. Furthermore, Looker provides additional applications through the Marketplace that can assist in effectively understanding and managing all your Looker content.

Looker provides a comprehensive content management framework to handle large volumes of dashboards and Looks, ensuring efficient organization, accessibility, and discoverability for users.

In this chapter, we're going to cover the following topics related to Looker content management elements:

- Exploring the Looker home page, favorites, and boards
- Organizing Looker folders
- Facilitate Looker exploration with Looker Marketplace applications
- Organizing the LookML environment

Technical requirements

There are no specific requirements or preparation steps for this chapter. We will continue working in our Looker instance.

Exploring the Looker home page, favorites, and boards

When on the Looker home page, you will see the menu (with **Explore**, **Develop**, and **Admin**) on the left, your favorite and recently viewed content in the center, and the **From Your Organization** section on the right.

The Looker home page is usually the place to start your Looker work. It is recommended to favorite some of your most used content so it appears on the home page and is easy to access.

While the home page is personalized for each user, Looker's boards enable teams to discover and access curated collections of dashboards and Looks. These assets, which are organized within folders, can be pinned to multiple boards for convenient access.

Getting ready

Go to the Looker home page using the URL (`your-instance-id`)`.looker.app/browse` (this URL structure works only for Looker Google Cloud core). You can also click on the Looker logo in the top-left corner of your Looker environment to go to the home page.

How to do it...

To add favorites, let's do the following:

1. When on the home page, find **Folders** and then click on **My Folder**. This is where the content we created previously (dashboards and Looks) is stored (if folders and the whole left-side section of the page are not visible, you might need to click on the "burger" menu button).

2. In **My folder**, near every piece of content, there is a heart icon that you can click to add the element to your favorites (*Figure 8.1*).

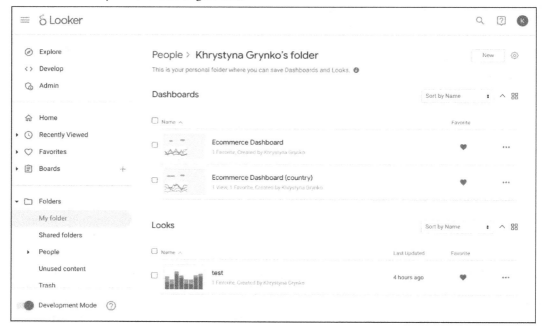

Figure 8.1 – My folder

3. Go back to the home page by clicking on **Home** on the left side of the page – now, you should see the content in **Your favorite content**. Note that you cannot modify the **Recently viewed by you** and **Recently viewed at your organization** sections as they are filled automatically with the content you consulted.

4. If you don't see what you need in your favorites and recently viewed content, you can search for it by clicking on the magnifying glass icon at the top-right corner of the page. Near the magnifying glass icon, there is a question mark icon as well – it provides links to the documentation and support.

Managing the "From Your Organization" section

As an admin, you can add useful links or messages you want to communicate to your Looker users. To do that, follow these steps:

1. On the home page, find the **From Your Organization** section.

2. Click +**Add New Card**.

3. Add some text for **Title**, as well as **Description**, **URL**, and **Image** (these three are optional), then click **Create** (*Figure 8.2*).

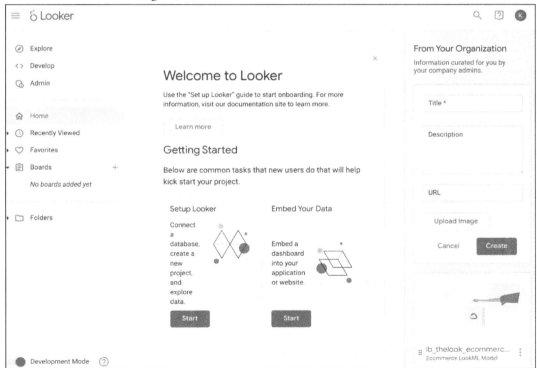

Figure 8.2 – From Your Organization

Here, in the bottom-right corner of the screenshot (*Figure 8.2*), you can see the link to the e-commerce Looker model that I added to have quick access to it. Be mindful that anything you add in this section will be shown to all Looker users, and some of them may not have LookML access.

Creating Boards

To create your board, let's do the following:

1. In the left section of the page, click on + next to **Boards**. Then, choose **Create New Board**.
2. Provide a name to your board – for example, `Ecommerce Board`.
3. You can organize the board by section; for example, let's add the following title and description to the first section: **Title**: `Ecommerce analysis - Users`. **Description**: `This section will contain an analysis of user demographics and behavior`
4. Click on **Add Content | Saved content**.
5. Browse **My Folder** and click on **Ecommerce Dashboard** (which you should have from previous chapters) – now it is added to your board.
6. Near the **Ecommerce Dashboard** element in your board, click on + to add other content or a URL (*Figure 8.3*).

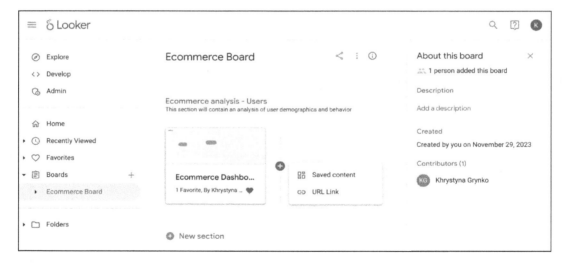

Figure 8.3 – Board

7. Add a link to your `users view` in the LookML project or the user table in BigQuery. Add a title and description for that. You can specify in the description that this element can only be accessible by LookML developers.

8. In the **About this board** section on the right, you can add the description of the board and who has contributed to it.

9. In front of the board name (**Ecommerce Board**), there is a share icon where you can provide access (**View** or **Manage/Edit**) to other users to work with them on this board.

10. The three-dots icon near the share icon gives you the possibility to delete the board or remove it from the list (by default, the board you create is included in the list under **Boards** in the left panel. The boards created by your colleagues will contain an **Add To My List** button so you can add them to the same list if needed).

11. The **i** icon opens the **About this Board** section.

How it works...

Looker's boards offer several benefits:

- **Custom home page**: Configure a board as a home page with curated content for your Looker users

- **Enriched information**: Enhance board content with links and descriptions for context and guidance.

- **Curation for teams**: Organize and share dashboards and Looks specific to your team's needs.

- **Multi-board pinning**: Easily access the same Looks or dashboards across multiple boards.

- **New user onboarding**: Guide new users with a dedicated onboarding board, directing them to relevant content.

- **Accessibility control**: Public boards are accessible to all, while private boards are restricted.

- **Access-level enforcement**: Respect existing access levels, ensuring users only see authorized content. Users will only see boards for which they have the View access level. To add dashboards and Looks to boards and provide helpful context, users need the **Manage Access, Edit** access level.

Looker's **From Your Organization** section on the home page can be used, for example, to do the following:

- Add some links to the training material

- Add some announcements about upcoming events, data outages, and newly added content

- Add contacts for internal support

See also

- Find and organize content: `https://cloud.google.com/looker/docs/find-and-organize-content`

- Presenting content with boards: `https://cloud.google.com/looker/docs/presenting-content`

Organizing Looker folders

Folders in Looker are another way to organize your content. They can be created by theme, team, department (such as HR, finance, marketing, etc.), or any other criteria relevant to your organization. By default, Looker contains the following folders:

- **My Folder**: So far, we have used this to save our content. Your personal folder is visible to Looker admins but not visible and editable by others unless you give them permission.

- **Shared Folders**: Your organization's folders that contain dashboards and Looks for specific groups of people.

- **People**: The **My Folder** area of your colleagues is visible to you if you are a Looker admin or you have been given permission to access the folder. Choose a name to see the dashboards and Looks a user created or saved to their folder. At this stage, there might be only our folder (if you haven't shared the Looker free trial with your colleagues).

- **Unused content** (**Admin**): Contains Looks and dashboards that people have not viewed in the last 90 days (3 months).

- **Trash** (**Admin**): Contains Looks and dashboards you have deleted.

Depending on your content, the **Folders** section might also contain the following folders: **LookML Dashboards** (contains dashboards that developers created using LookML), **Embed Users** (dashboards and Looks that this person saved to their personal folder when using an embedded version of Looker), and **Embed Groups** (dashboards and Looks that people using an embedded version of Looker shared with this group).

Getting ready

When on the home page, in the left-hand navigation menu, go to **Folders**. The **All Folders** page will open.

How to do it...

To work with the folders, you should do the following:

1. On the **All Folders** page, choose one of the main default folders; for example, click on **Shared Folders**.

2. Imagine you are working for an analytics agency that provides reports to different customers in different industries. In this case, your shared folder (which is used throughout the agency) might contain different folders by industry. In the top-right corner, next to **Your organization's folders**, click on **New | Folder** (*Figure 8.4*).

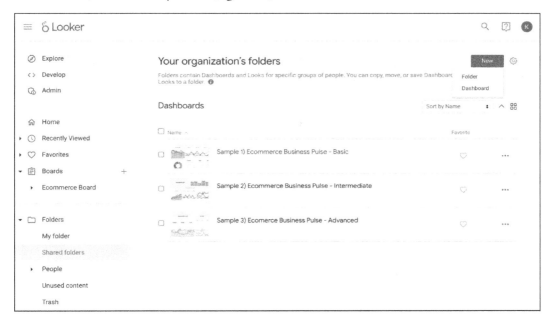

Figure 8.4 – Folders

3. Name your folder (for example, `Retail`, for all your retail customers). Click on **Create Folder,** and the empty **Retail** folder will open.

4. Inside the **Retail** folder, click on **New | Folder** to create a subfolder inside the **Retail** folder.

5. Name your subfolder, for example, `Customer A`, then click on **Create Folder**.

6. In the left navigation menu, find **Folders | My folder**.

7. In **My Folder**, click on the three dots near the element (dashboard or Look) that you want to move to your **Customer A** folder. After clicking on the three dots, you will see the options to rename, add to a board, move, copy, and move to trash. Click on **Move**.

8. In the **Move Dashboard** pop-up window, click on **Shared**, then click on **Retail,** and then **Customer A.**

9. Click **OK** to finalize the dashboard migration from one folder to another.

Managing Access to Folders

To manage access to folders, let's do the following:

1. Go to **Folders | Shared Folders | Retail | Customer A.**

2. In the top-right corner, click on the gear icon, then choose **Manage access.**

3. Choose **A custom list of users** to add one user or a group of users. The groups of users can be created in the Admin section, which we will discuss later in the book (*Chapter 9*).

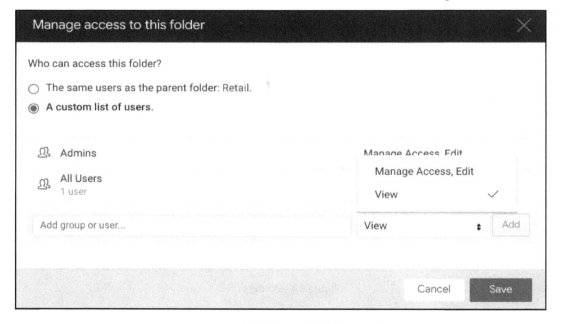

Figure 8.5 – Access to Folders

4. You can provide the following accesses to users: **View** or **Manage Access, Edit** (*Figure 8.5*).

There's more...

You might want to have some kind of intermediate folder in the **Shared Folder** to add all your elements there to be verified by another colleague. For example, you can create a **Content to be verified** folder where you place your work; when your colleague verifies that everything is correct and is working, they can place the content into the industry folders.

It is up to you/your team to find your own best practices for Looker content management.

See also

- Deleted and unused content for admins: `https://cloud.google.com/looker/docs/admin-spaces`

- Organizing and managing access to content: `https://cloud.google.com/looker/docs/organizing-spaces`

Facilitate Looker exploration with Looker Marketplace applications

The Looker Marketplace is a place where you can find different applications, plugins, additional visualizations, and other pre-built Looker elements. For example, you can find there a **Calendar Heatmap** visualization, which is not available in Looker by default. You can also find the Google Analytics LookML block, so you don't have to build the model from scratch for a typical GA dataset.

This section will explore two Looker Marketplace applications that can provide helpful tools for your Looker environment to promote content discovery and code organization.

Getting ready

The Marketplace is not available in the free trial by default; you need to activate it. To do that in Looker, go to the **Admin** section. In the **Platform** drop-down list, click on **Marketplace** and then on **I agree to Marketplace Terms and Conditions**. After your page is refreshed, you will see the Marketplace icon in the top-right corner near the search icon.

How to do it...

Let's add our first application from the Marketplace:

1. In Looker, in the top-right corner, click on the **Marketplace** icon (*Figure 8.6*).

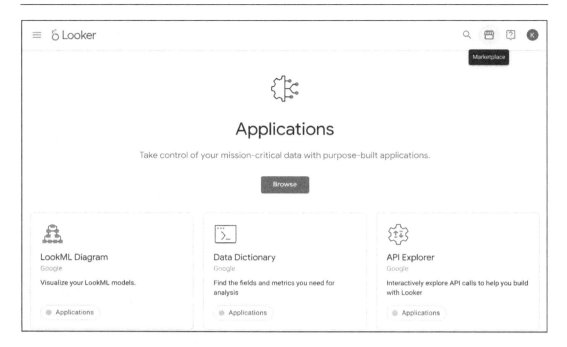

Figure 8.6 – Marketplace

2. In the **Applications** section, click on **LookML Diagram**.

3. On the LookML diagram page, click on **Install | Default Installation method**.

4. Read and accept the license agreement.

5. Click on **Agree and Continue**.

6. Choose your db/dwh connection.

7. Once you see **Installation created for LookML Diagram**, click **Open**.

8. In the LookML Diagram interface, open the LookML model you want to explore.

9. Then, choose one of the tables to see how it is connected with others.

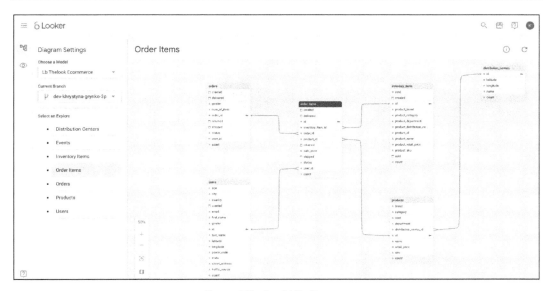

Figure 8.7 – LookML diagram

10. For example, the **Order Items** table is connected to many other tables and it might be important to know how to work with this table (*Figure 8.7*).

11. Click on any field to see the information about this field (details and code).

12. From the field information window, open it on the right, and you can click on **Go to LookML** or **Explore with Field**.

The LookML Diagram application helps you to understand the organization of your model and views and the connections between the views within your model.

Working with Data Dictionary

Let's add another application to our Looker environment – Data Dictionary:

1. In the top-right corner, click on the **Marketplace** icon.

2. In the **Applications** section of the **Marketplace** page, click on **Data Dictionary**.

3. On the **Data Dictionary** page, click on **Install | install**.

4. Read and accept the license agreement.

5. Click on **Agree and Continue**.

6. Choose your db/dwh connection.

7. Once you see **Installation created for Data Dictionary**, click **Open** next to **Data Dictionary**.

8. You can now explore and filter your fields to see available data. By clicking on **View Options**, you can add (or hide) columns on your Data Dictionary table (*Figure 8.8*).

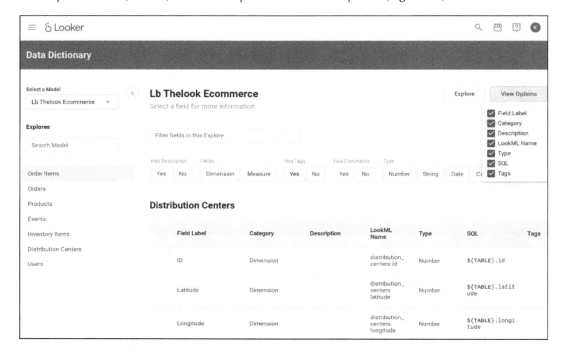

Figure 8.8 – Data Dictionary

9. By clicking on a field, for example, **ID**, the **Details** and **Comments** section will open on the right. You can add comments to share more info about the field. Note that these comments are unique to fields in the Data Dictionary and are not saved to any LookML description.

The Looker Data Dictionary extension provides an interface for searching through Looker fields and descriptions.

There's more...

You can find the LookML Diagram and Looker Data Dictionary applications in the **Applications** section in the left-navigation Looker menu (*Figure 8.9*).

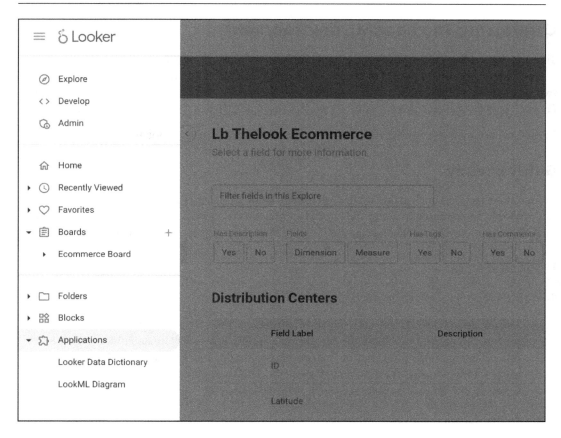

Figure 8.9 – Applications

To delete or configure your applications, click on the Marketplace icon | **Manage**.

See also

- Configuring the LookML Diagram: `https://cloud.google.com/looker/docs/lookml-diagram-configuring`

- Using the Looker Data Dictionary: `https://cloud.google.com/looker/docs/using-looker-data-dictionary`

- Organizing Looker Content by Data Clymer: `https://dataclymer.com/blog/organizing-looker-content/`

Organizing the LookML environment

The LookML environment is accessed by significantly fewer users than the previous features discussed in this chapter. A LookML project is a restricted place managed by LookML developers/data engineers to prepare Looker Explores for self-service analytics. However, it is extremely important to keep your LookML projects well organized to make the work of your LookML developers easier and more efficient.

In this section, we will review the best practices for your LookML project organization.

Getting ready

In the left navigation panel, make sure **Development Mode** is activated and go to **Develop | Projects | lb_thelook_ecommerce** to get to the LookML project we explored previously in this book (you might have named your LookML project differently; find the one you used throughout this book).

How to do it...

To organize your LookML environment well, do the following:

1. Use folders in LookML projects to organize the content. You have basic *views* and *models* folders, but you can create a new folder by clicking on + in **File Browser | Create Folder** (*Figure 8.10*) or by clicking on the three dots near an existing folder (to create a subfolder). You can always move folders by using the drag-and-drop method. In some cases, LookML developers decide to organize views using subfolders, such as the following:

    - One subfolder for "base" views (principal views based on original tables)

    - Another subfolder for "refined" views, derived tables, and modified base views

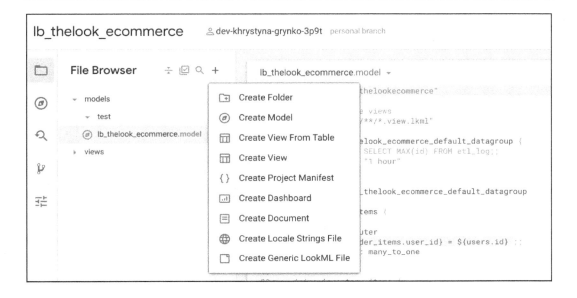

Figure 8.10 – Folders

2. Implement consistent naming for LookML files and elements. Use descriptive names that accurately reflect their purpose, for example, `siteA_customers.view` or `explore_orders_by_product.lkml`.

3. Utilize substitution operators ($) to avoid repetitive code. This makes your LookML more concise and maintainable.

4. Document your code with clear and concise comments. Explain complex calculations, data sources, and dependencies for future reference.

5. Use Git or another version control system to track changes, revert to previous versions, and collaborate efficiently in LookML. Make sure you follow the Git management best practices, such as the following:

    • Keep commits small and focused on specific types of changes

    • Write clear and concise commit messages

    • Isolate changes and reduce conflicts by creating branches for specific strategic changes

    • Stay up to date – regularly pull changes from the main branch

    • Send your code for reviews through Git

6. Establish LookML style guidelines for your team. This fosters consistency and simplifies collaboration.

7. Utilize LookML tools and scripts for tasks such as testing, linting, and deployment. This saves time and reduces human error.

See also

- Managing LookML files and folders: `https://cloud.google.com/looker/docs/creating-project-files`

- Setting up and testing a Git connection: `https://cloud.google.com/looker/docs/setting-up-git-connection`

- What are Git version control best practices?: `https://about.gitlab.com/topics/version-control/version-control-best-practices/`

9

Administering and Monitoring Looker

Administering Looker and monitoring its usage is important to your Looker journey.

The Looker **Admin** section in Looker's interface is your command center for managing your organization's seamless and effective data analytics experience. Within its walls lies a vast array of tools and functionalities, carefully crafted to empower Looker's administrators with the following administration functions: **General**, **System Activity**, **Users**, **Database**, **Alerts & Schedules**, **Platform**, and **Authentication**.

Some administrative functions can be performed from your Google Cloud project where your Looker (Google Cloud core) instance sits: view and edit instance details of the instance, manage user access, set up a custom domain, leverage VPC Service Controls (for certain instance types), enable CMEK (should be set up before the instance creation), import or export data, manage maintenance policies, and delete instances.

In this chapter, we are going to cover the following topics related to administering and monitoring your Looker instance within the Looker environment:

- Configuring principal settings
- Managing users in a granular way
- Analyzing the system activity
- Exploring advanced settings

The management of Looker via Google Cloud is not covered in this book. Instead, we will focus on the Looker Admin page to manage settings within the Looker application itself. Refer to this documentation page to explore the administrative aspects of Looker accessible through Google Cloud: `https://cloud.google.com/looker/docs/looker-core-admin-console`.

> **Note**
>
> You can use Terraform to automate the provisioning and configuration of key aspects of Looker: `https://registry.terraform.io/providers/hashicorp/google/latest/docs/resources/looker_instance`

Technical requirements

To perform administrative tasks within the Looker instance, you need the Looker Admin (`roles/looker.admin`) IAM role on the Google Cloud project in which the instance was created. If you continue using the same Looker instance that you created and used throughout this book, you should have full admin access to the Google Cloud project and the Looker instance.

Configuring principal settings

In this section, we will delve into the most critical and frequently used Admin settings within Looker. We will begin with the **Database** pages, having already touched upon them briefly. Following that, we will explore the **General** and **Alerts & Schedules** pages in detail. The remaining **Admin** pages will be addressed later in this chapter.

Getting ready

Go to the Looker interface, click on the menu button, and then click on **Admin**.

How to do it...

Let's dive into the main administrative panels, starting with the familiar **Database** section:

1. In **Admin**, click on the **Database** drop-down list and choose **Connections**.

2. In **Connections**, you can choose **Edit** or **Test your existing database/data warehouse connections** and add new connections by clicking on **Add Connection**. To connect Looker to your database or data warehouse, select the type of authentication you want Looker to use to access your database: you have the option to configure OAuth, a service account, or **Application Default Credentials** to authenticate to your database. If you encounter connection errors in your Looker Explores or are aware of significant changes made by your database administrator that might impact the connection, it is recommended to test and potentially edit your connection settings in the **Admin's Connections** panel.

3. In the **Database** drop-down list, choose **Queries**. On the **Queries** page, you can find a table with details about the latest 50 requests sent to your database through this Looker instance. The **Details** button on every line of the table gives a lot of information about the query, such as **Source**, **User**, and **Connection**. Some contain SQL query code in the **SQL** tab as well. Click on **Details** of any query to discover the available information.

4. Click on the **Database** drop-down list and choose **Persistent Derived Tables (PDTs)**. PDTs are derived tables stored in a database, automatically refreshed on a schedule you control. The **Persistent Derived Table** page in the Admin's **Database** panel allows you to troubleshoot PDTs in development and production. To filter what PDTs you want to troubleshoot, you have multiple options:

    I.   Click on **All Connections** to choose the database connections you want to focus on (PDTs only for a specific database) – if you don't have a drop-down list, it means you have only one connection set up.

    II.   Use the search bar in the top-right corner to search for a PDT of interest.

    III. Click on the **filter** icon (inverted pyramid) near the search bar to filter what PDTs you want to check.

5. In the **Database** drop-down list, choose **Datagroups**. Datagroups are used to assign a caching policy for Explores and a persistence strategy for PDTs. If you have already set up a datagroup in LookML, you might see it on the **Database Datagroups** page. If you click on the gear icon in the **Actions** column of this datagroup line, you can do the following:

    I.   Reset **Cache** (to clear the saved results for all Explores based on a specific datagroup).

    II.   Trigger a datagroup (to clear results and rebuild pre-built queries (PDTs) linked to the datagroup).

    III. Click on **LookML** to go to the LookML editor and debug this datagroup if needed.

6. To assign a caching policy for Explores or to specify a persistence strategy for PDTs, you can use the **Datagroup** parameter in LookML.

Exploring the General panel

Let's explore the Admin's **General** panel now:

1. Click on the **Looker** menu, then click on **Admin**.

2. Open the Admin's **General** drop-down list and click on **Localization**. There are only two parameters in **Localization**:

    • **Locale**: Set up the Looker interface language here. If nothing is set up, the default parameter is **en**. This parameter can also be set up at the user/user group levels (**Admin -> Users -> Add User...**). User or user group settings override instance settings.

    • **Number format**: To configure what your numbers look like in Looker, there are three options available. This parameter can be modified at the user level as well.

3. Model localization often occurs in conjunction with admin localization settings. Model localization lets you adapt your model's labels and descriptions to match the language and customs of your users. To configure the localization in your LookML model, check this page:

   `https://cloud.google.com/looker/docs/model-localization`.

4. In Admin's **General** section, click on **Internal Help Resources**. Click on the toggle button near **Enable Internal Help Resources** in the **Help** menu and, modify the **Organization Name** and **Enter Markdown Below** (Markdown lets you easily add formatting to text such as headings, lists, and bold) sections to guide your users on utilizing helpful internal resources (*Figure 9.1*).

Figure 9.1 – Internal Help Resources

5. Now go to another part of Admin's **General** section – **Homepage**. This is where you can set up a homepage for your entire organization. It can be a standard homepage or a specific Looker URL (for example, a URL of the **Board** page). The homepage can be adapted to specific users as well. It is configured in the Admin's **Users** section. To set a default homepage for specific groups or individuals, head over to the **User Attributes** section and edit the **landing_page** user attribute.

6. The biggest section of the Admin's **General** panel is **Settings**. Let's click on it to explore some of the available configurations in this section:

- **Application Time Zone**: This is the main time zone of your Looker app. The scheduled Looks will use this time zone. Change it to the time zone of your choice and click on **Update**. You can enable user-specific time zones later, in **Settings**, if needed, then change time zones in **Admin** -> **Users**.

- **Default Private Personal Folders**: With this option, you can make a personal user's folder invisible to others (which is not the case by default). If you want to make any changes, don't forget to click on **Update** to save the changes.

- **New Account Notification**: You can enable this to make sure that all the admins receive a notification when a new user is added and the account is activated. If you want to make any changes, don't forget to click on **Update** to save the changes.

- **Cookie Notification Banner**: Activate this if you are working in the EU.

- **Default Visualization Colors**: You can choose a color palette for your Looker visualizations or create a new one (with your company colors, for example).

- In the **Data Policy** subsection of the **General** settings, you can prevent some actions from happening. For example, with **Public URLs** disabled, you can prevent the public sharing of Looks. With **Block Formulas and Macros in CSV and Excel Files** enabled, everything that can be read as macros or formulas in exported CSV/Excel files will be escaped.

7. Review the **General** settings one by one to understand whether you need any of these for your Looker environment configuration.

Exploring the Alerts & Schedules panel

Now let's see what we can do in the Admin's **Alerts & Schedules** panel:

1. You can set up alerts and review **Alert History**. Alerts in Looker give you the possibility to send a message to a recipient or a group of recipients whenever there is a suspicious/unusual event that happens with your data. Alerts are configured in **Dashboards**, but in Admin's **Alerts & Schedules** panel, you can explore the **Alerts** dashboard in the **Alerts** section and the history of running, complete, and failed alerts in **Alerts History**.

2. You can review what has been scheduled in **Schedule** and see what worked and what failed in **Schedule History**. Schedules let you regularly send Looks or dashboards to a recipient or a group of recipients. In **Schedules**, in the **Alerts & Schedules** section of the Admin menu, you have the list of all the schedules in the Looker instance. In **Schedule History**, you have information about running, successful, and failed schedules to check whether anything needs troubleshooting.

3. You can find the information about the email that has been scheduled from the Looker interface in **Scheduled Emails** – the place to manage the emailed data policy (to configure whether users can send data only, a link only, or data and links) and to review the external recipients and the email senders.

There's more...

Remember that some of the administrative functions can be done from the Google Cloud console:

`https://cloud.google.com/looker/docs/looker-core-admin-console`

See also

- Database pages: `https://cloud.google.com/looker/docs/admin-panel-database-pages`
- General pages: `https://cloud.google.com/looker/docs/admin-panel-general-pages`
- Alerts & Schedules: `https://cloud.google.com/looker/docs/admin-panel-alerts-and-schedules-pages`

Managing users in a granular way

In Looker, managing who has access to your data and analytical tools is crucial for maintaining security and ensuring efficient collaboration. This section dives into the nuances of user management within Looker, guiding you through the various methods of granting access and controlling permissions.

As of today, Looker (Google Cloud core) integrates with the Google Cloud IAM service to authenticate and authorize users (other options will be available later). Once users are added through Google Cloud IAM, the **Users** panel in Looker's Admin page provides fine-grained control through roles and groups. You can assign roles, which define a set of permissions, to individual users or groups, allowing you to tailor access levels to specific needs.

Service accounts, which can be added inside Looker's interface, differ from user accounts. They are not tied to individuals but rather applications that utilize Looker APIs. Whenever you need an application to connect to Looker APIs, you will add your service account in the Looker Admin's **Users** panel.

Looker offers flexible authentication options, including support for SAML, OpenID Connect, and other third-party connections.

Getting ready

Open two tabs in your browser – one with the Google Cloud console (`https://console.cloud.google.com/`) and one with your Looker instance (you can always find your instance URL here: `https://console.cloud.google.com/looker/instances`).

How to do it...

To add a user to your Looker instance and assign them a specific role, let's do the following:

1. In the Google Cloud console, find the **IAM and Admin** service (search for it in a search bar or in the menu by clicking on the burger menu button in the top-left corner).

2. On the first page (IAM) of the IAM and Admin service, in the **PERMISSION** tab, click on **Grant Access**.

3. In **New Principals**, add the email address of the person you want to add to your Looker account and choose the **Looker instance user** role (*Figure 9.2*). Other options available are **Looker Admin** (the role you have), **Looker Viewer** (to give read-only access to Looker resources), and **Looker Service Agent** (these agents exist for APIs you use and appear in project settings such as policies and audit logs).

Figure 9.2 – Cloud IAM

4. In your Looker instance, in Admin's **Authentication** panel, click on **Google**, and choose the default role for new users (**Developer** can modify LookML, **User** or **Standard User** can work with Explores, and **Viewer** can only view the content elements). Let's choose **User** and click on **Update**.

5. Copy and send the Looker instance URL (**Google Cloud console -> Looker**) to the person you provided access to. After this person connects for the first time, you will see their email in the Looker Admin's **Users** panel (the **Add Service Account** button on the **Users** page in the Admin's **Users** panel gives you the possibility to create special accounts for automation and integrations, but not regular user accounts, which can be added through Google Cloud IAM only).

> **Important note**
>
> Suppose the person you provided access to is outside your organization (with a different email domain). In that case, you might need to provide access to this domain (if you have an email domain allowlist restriction): go to **Google Cloud console**, find Looker, click on your Looker instance's name, and then click on **Edit and modify Email Domain Allowlist**. The **Email Domain Allowlist** setting restricts the email domains where Looker users can send content.

6.   Go to the Looker Admin's **Users** panel to check whether the user you added is there (*Figure 9.3*) and has the role **User**.

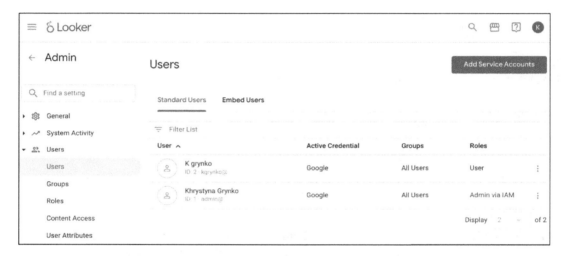

Figure 9.3 – Users

7.   Now go to **Groups** (**Admin** -> **Users** -> **Groups**) and click on **Add Group**.

8.   Name the group `Marketing`.

9.   In this `Marketing` group, click on **Add Members**.

10. Add the new Looker user to this group: search for an email, then click **Add Members** (you can add multiple members).

11. Go to **Roles**. Roles combine permissions (what users can do) and data access (what they can see) based on model sets and permission sets.

12. In **Roles**, click on **New Permission Set**.

13. Give the new permission set a name (**Advanced Explorer**) and check the following boxes: `access_data`, `see_looks`, `explore`, `create_table_calculations`, `create_custom_fields`, `can_create_forecast`, `save_content`. Then scroll and click on **New Permission Set** to create one.

14. Go back to **Roles** and click on **New Model Set**.

15. Name it **Ecommerce Model** and check the box near your `lb_thelook_ecommerce` model.

16. Click on **New Model Set** to create one.

17. In **Users -> Roles**, click on **New Role**.

18. Name it **Marketing Ecommerce Explorers** and choose **Advanced Explorer** for **Permission Set**, **Ecommerce Model** for **Model Set**, and **Marketing** for **Groups**.

19. Click on **New Role** to create a new role and click **Confirm**.

20. Click **Cancel** to go back to the **Roles** page.

Managing Content Accesses

To manage the user's access to content, let's do the following:

1. Go to **Admin -> Users -> Content Access**.

2. Choose the content you want to restrict access to (for example, **Shared -> Retail -> Customer A**).

3. Click on **Manage Access**.

4. In the pop-up window, choose **A custom list of users**.

5. In the search bar of **Manage access to this folder**, find a new user and assign them the **Manage Access, Edit** role (*Figure 9.4*).

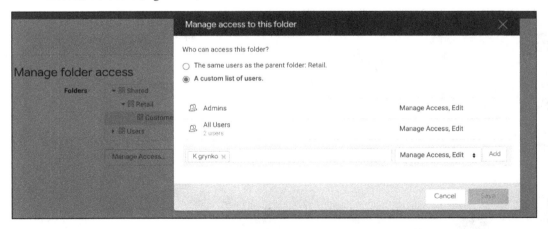

Figure 9.4 – Content access

6. Click on **Add**, then **Save**.

Managing User Attributes

User attributes are additional user parameters that can be set up in the Admin's **Users** panel and used in LookML to limit access to certain dimensions or measures according to these user parameters. Let's discover how to use **User Attributes**:

1. Go to the **Admin** -> **Users** drop-down list and then **User Attributes**.

2. Click **Create User Attribute**.

3. Give it a name (for example, `department`).

4. In **User Access**, click **None**, and in **Hide Values**, click **No**.

5. Click **Save**.

6. Two tabs will appear: **Group Values** and **User Values**.

7. In **Group Values**, click on **+Add Group**.

8. Choose **Marketing group**, which we created previously, and add **marketing** as a value.

9. Click **Save**. Now, all the users in the **Marketing group** will have a user attribute department set for **marketing**. You can add other groups and set up their attributes.

10. The attributes can be set on the individual user level as well. Click on the **User Values** tab in your **Department** user attribute. In the drop-down list, choose your admin's email and click on **Set value for User**.

11. Set the value to `data` and click **Save** (*Figure 9.5*).

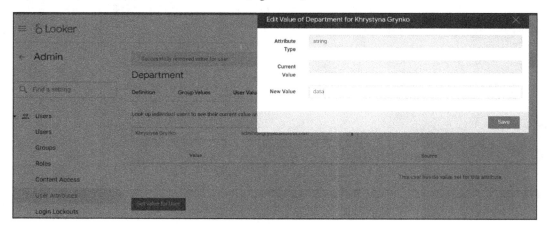

Figure 9.5 – User attributes

12. Now let's use **User Attributes** in our LookML project. Go to **Menu** -> **Develop** -> **Projects** -> **LookML projects**.

13. Click on the `lb_thelook_ecommerce` LookML project.

14. Open `lb_thelook_ecommerce.model`, add the following code (for example, before the first **explore** block), and click **Save Changes**:

```
access_grant: can_view_ecommerce_data {
  user_attribute: department
  allowed_values: [ "marketing","data" ]
}
```

15. Open `orders.view`, and after the `sql_table_name` line, add the following code and click **Save Changes**:

```
required_access_grants: [can_view_ecommerce_data]
```

16. As always, you can click on **Validate LookML** in the top-right corner, then on **Commit Changes & Push** to make the changes visible to everyone.

How it works...

In the previous section, in the **User Attributes** exercise, we restricted access to the `orders view` to users that have the attributes listed in the `access_grant` parameter at the model level. This is another reusable Looker parameter to facilitate your LookML work and secure your data. The `required_access_grants` parameter, which pairs with the model-level `access_grant` parameter, isn't just for views. It can be used across various Looker elements such as Explores, joins, dimensions, and more: `https://cloud.google.com/looker/docs/reference/param-view-required-access-grants`.

There's more...

In the Admin's **User** panel, you can see the **Login Lockouts** subsection. Looker locks out accounts for 5 minutes after 4 failed logins from the same IP. Even with the correct credentials, you can't log in from that IP during the lockout. This applies per user and IP, not across them. Lockouts don't affect signed embed users. In **Login Lockouts**, you can find locked accounts and unlock them before the 5-minute lockout ends. Read more about it in the documentation: `https://cloud.google.com/looker/docs/admin-panel-users-login-lockouts`.

In the Admin's **Authentication** panel, in **Sessions**, you can set up different configurations to control users' login sessions and provide additional security for your Looker instance. Read more about it in the documentation: `https://cloud.google.com/looker/docs/admin-panel-authentication-sessions`

See also

- Manage user access to a Looker instance: `https://cloud.google.com/looker/docs/looker-core-manage-users`

Analyzing system activity

Looker offers an internal tool called **System Activity**, powered by a dedicated LookML model connected to Looker's underlying application database. This tool provides detailed information about your Looker instance, including saved Looks and dashboards, user data, query history, and performance statistics. It's important to note that the amount of data collected and how long it's stored are subject to system limitations.

Looker's **System Activity** section contains the following subsections: **User Activity**, **Content Activity**, **Database Performance**, **Instance Performance**, **Performance Recommendations**, and **Errors and Broken Content**.

In this section, we will explore **System Activity** reports and how you can customize them.

Getting ready

Click on Looker's menu button (in the top-left corner of the Looker interface) and then click on **Admin**. In **Admin**, find the **System Activity** section.

How to do it...

Let's walk through different **System Activity** reports:

1. In Admin's **System Activity** section, click on **User Activity**. **User Activity** reports show how users interact with Looker's interface. In this report, you will find information about different types of users, their weekly engagement, the top dashboard builders, and so on. You can exclude Looker support that helped you with your Looker instance by using the **Looker Employee: is No** filter (*Figure 9.6*).

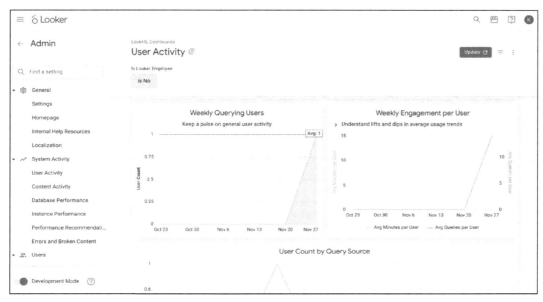

Figure 9.6 – User Activity report

2. Now click on the **Content Activity** report in Admin's **System Activity** section. It is very important information that helps you understand how your Looker content is being used and whether it makes sense to make some changes to it (like, for example, deleting unused dashboards).

3. Now, let's go to the **Database Performance** report. Mark the **Results from Cache** tile. It might give you some useful information on how the cache is used and whether you should optimize your caching policy, for example, by specifying a longer cache retention policy at the LookML Explore level and the LookML model level.

4. When you click on the **Instance Performance** report, you can discover what is scheduled and downloaded often in your Looker instance. These two activities can potentially result in reduced performance of the Looker server.

5. **Performance Recommendations** provides recommendations for dashboards and Explores. This report might contain some important warnings about what should be fixed (at this stage of your Looker usage, you might have no recommendations, and that is all right).

6. The **Errors and Broken Content** section communicates problems with dashboards, schedules, Looks, PDTs, and query sources.

Creating System Activity reports

You can create your own dashboards based on the **System Activity** data. To do that, let's do the following:

1. Go to one of the reports, for example, the **Content Activity** report.

2. Click on the three dots near one of the dashboard tiles, then click on **Explore from here** (*Figure 9.7*).

Figure 9.7 – Content Activity – Explore from here

3. This will bring you to one of the underlying **System Activity** Explores, where you can choose the columns you need; click **Run** and save your query as a Look or to a new or existing dashboard (*Figure 9.8*).

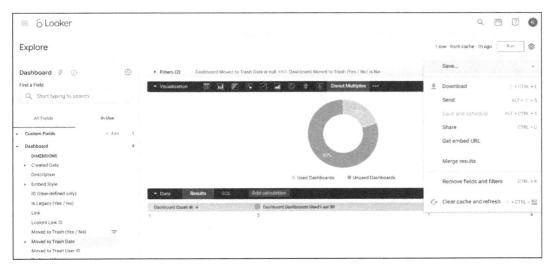

Figure 9.8 – System Activity Explore

4. You might want to explore other System Activity Explores as well. To do this, click the Looker menu button in the top - left corner, then navigate to **Explore**. In the search panel, enter '**System Activity**' to see available options like API Usage, Content Usage, DB Connection, and more.

The System Activity Explores provide the data you need to create a customized dashboard for detailed insights into your Looker instance's usage. You might want to add this dashboard to a specific folder or board for better organization.

How it works...

Looker automatically stores **System Activity** data internally, but most tables are regularly cleared to manage storage space. For instance, the **History** table only keeps data for the past 90 days. Some tables have even stricter retention policies.

Querying **System Activity** data directly through SQL Runner is not possible due to limited permissions for Looker's internal database.

See also

- System Activity pages: `https://cloud.google.com/looker/docs/system-activity-pages`

- Using the System Activity Explores: `https://cloud.google.com/looker/docs/usage-reports-with-system-activity-explores#using_the_system_activity_explores`

- Understanding query performance metrics: `https://cloud.google.com/looker/docs/query-performance-metrics`

Exploring advanced settings

In this section, we'll work with the **Platform** Admin's panel. Looker's **Platform** pages in Admin empower you to do the following:

- Extend functionality: Build custom apps (Actions, Extensions) and access Marketplace extensions
- Control access: Manage API access, embedding options, and extension availability
- Customize Looker: Define themes, configure email notifications, and personalize the user experience

These pages unlock Looker's potential for administrators and developers to create a secure, tailored environment for your users.

Click on Looker's menu button (in the top-left corner of Looker's interface) and then click on **Admin**. In Admin, find the **Platform** section.

Let's look at different sections in the Admin's **Platform** panel, starting with the one we explored previously:

- **Marketplace**: Earlier in this book, we activated **Marketplace** in the dedicated **Marketplace** section, and a Marketplace icon subsequently appeared in the top-right corner of the interface. In this **Marketplace** section, we can activate Marketplace, auto install some supporting Looker-built applications (at the time of writing, only API Explorer is available), auto-update some Looker applications – you might see applications we are familiar with there: LookML Diagram and Data Dictionary. Let's do the following:

    I. Turn on the **Auto Install** feature by clicking its corresponding toggle switch (we will need the API explorer later in this book).

    II. Click the toggle switch to the right of **Auto Update Looker Applications** to enable it.

> **Important Note**
>
> At the time of writing, the Looker Marketplace isn't supported on Looker instances using private IP networks (either exclusively or in combination with a public IP). Note that the availability of certain Platform sections might depend on your Looker instance version `https://cloud.google.com/looker/docs/looker-core-admin-looker`.

- **Visualizations**: If you are not happy with the visualization types provided by Looker, you can always add a custom JavaScript visualization in the **Visualizations** section by providing a URL. You can also get a new visualization from the Marketplace (created by a verified provider) or add a visualization parameter to your LookML project's manifest file.

- **SMTP** stands for **Simple Mail Transfer Protocol**. The default setup means you use Looker's email service for all the emails sent from Looker (content, notifications, password reset, etc.). In the **SMTP** section, by clicking on **Use customer mail settings**, you can specify a different email service if, for example, required by your organization.

- **Extension Framework**: In this section, you can enable or disable the framework. Enabled by default, this feature empowers developers to create and run custom applications within Looker itself. Additionally, it unlocks the potential of the Looker Marketplace, allowing the installation and use of valuable extensions such as Data Dictionary. We will talk about the Extension Framework later in the book.

- **Embed**: The **Embed** page lets you adjust how Looker content looks and works when embedded in other tools. We will explore this functionality later in this book.

- **BI Connectors**: In this section, you can enable or disable Looker connections to non-Looker BI services (such as Google Sheets, for example).

- **API**: In this section, you can specify the API host URL. It tells users how to reach your Looker API. If Looker installation is behind a load balancer, use the user-facing domain name, not the server's name. If no path is specified by you, Looker uses the default API URL. Explore the Looker API Explorer extension on the Looker Marketplace. This extension offers a convenient and integrated way to discover the methods and types within the Looker SDK.

- **Actions**: In this section, you can add or activate the available Actions Hub. We already explored Actions in one of the previous chapters. At the time of writing, there are not a lot of third-party Actions available, but they should be added later. The Looker Action Hub is not available for Looker instances that use a private network connection.

See also

- Admin settings – Platform pages: `https://cloud.google.com/looker/docs/admin-panel-platform-pages`

- Administer a Looker instance: `https://cloud.google.com/looker/docs/looker-core-admin-looker`

10

Preparing to Develop Looker Applications

Looker shines in seamlessly integrating with other applications. Its robust features let you programmatically integrate Looker into your internal systems or build custom applications around it, unlocking a world of data possibilities.

This chapter provides a comprehensive overview of essential elements for Looker application development. Instead of delving into specific steps (which would necessitate a whole book!), we'll equip you with a curated list of links to detailed documentation, empowering you to dive deeper and build amazing Looker apps.

In this chapter, we're going to cover the following topics:

- Understanding Looker APIs
- Embedding Looker
- Exploring the Looker extension framework
- Exploring components
- Exploring the Looker Marketplace

Understanding Looker APIs

Application Programming Interfaces (APIs) are like digital bridges that connect different software applications, enabling them to communicate and exchange data efficiently. Looker's API unlocks nearly everything Looker can do via a user-friendly REST API using JSON. You can run queries, manage users, schedule reports, and build custom tools—all through code. Empowering developers with options, the API supports both direct HTTPS requests and seamless integration through language-specific SDKs. Looker's API Explorer is an extension that helps you to start exploring Looker's API. You can access it directly from the **Applications** menu if you have the extension installed or install it from the Marketplace. The public version is available on the Looker Developer Portal.

In this section, we will work with Looker's API Explorer. The API Explorer lets you explore the Looker SDK as well. A **Software Development Kit (SDK)** is a toolbox for developers to use on a specific platform. It includes pre-built code, APIs, documentation, samples, and debugging tools to build apps quickly and efficiently. The Looker SDKs provide a convenient way to communicate with the Looker API available on your Looker server.

Getting ready

Make sure the Marketplace is activated for your Looker instance by locating the Marketplace icon in the top - right corner. If it is not there, go to **Admin -> Platform-> Marketplace** and accept the terms and conditions to activate it.

How to do it...

To start working with the API Explorer, let's install it first:

1. Click on the Marketplace icon in the top-right corner of your Looker instance (*Figure 10.1*).

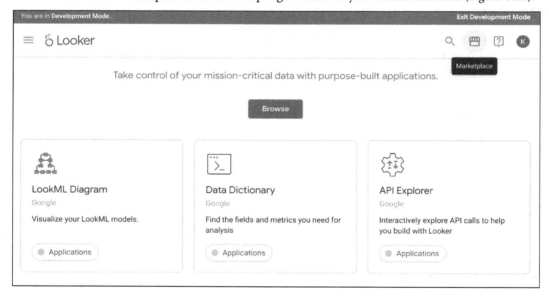

Figure 10.1 – API Explorer in the Marketplace

2. On the Marketplace page, find **API Explorer** and click on it.
3. On the API Explorer page, click on **+Install**, then from the drop-down list, choose **+Install** again.
4. Accept the license agreement, then click on **Agree and Continue**.

5. Choose your db/dwh connection (`thelook_ecommerce` in our case).

6. The API Explorer is now installed!

Working with API Explorer: Create Folders

Now, let's use the API Explorer to test API calls for managing folders in Looker:

1. Click on the **Looker Marketplace** icon, then click on **Manage**.

2. Click on **Open** to the right of **API Explorer** to open the extension.

3. On the API Explorer page, you will see the detailed API documentation on Looker API methods and types. Methods are actions you can take, while types define the data involved in those actions.

4. Scroll down through **Methods** and find the **Folder** section. Open the drop-down list by clicking on **Folder**, then click **Create Folder** (this API method explains how to programmatically create a folder in your Looker instance without using Looker's UI).

5. When on the **Create Folder** method page, you can find plenty of useful information about this method: for example, in the **Declarations** sections, you can find examples of code in different programming languages.

6. On the **Create Folder** method page, in the top-right corner, find the **Run It** button and click on it. The **Run It** environment gives you the possibility to test the Looker API methods.

7. In the **Request** tab, add `Test Folder` as the name of your future folder, and as a `parent_id`, add 1 this is the ID of our shared folder). Then, check the box next to **I understand that this API endpoint will change data**. Finally, click **Run** (*Figure 10.2*).

Figure 10.2 – Run It API Explorer

8. Go to the **Response** tab to make sure there are no errors. Click on **SDK Call** to see how the full code looks.

9. Click on the burger menu button in the top-left corner and go to **Folders** -> **Shared folders** to check whether your new **Test Folder** was created

Working with API Explorer: Create Queries

Let's now create a Looker query and get the data from this query through the API:

1. In the **Methods** panel of the API Explorer, search for the Create Query method.

2. Open it by clicking on **Create Query**, then click on **Run It**. In the **Request** tab, add the following parameters to the request: the model's name ("model": "lb_thelook_ecommerce"), the view's name ("view": "orders"), and the fields you want to get ("fields": ["orders.status", "orders.count"]). You might have different model/view names in your case, so make sure to enter the names you have. With this method, we create a query that will later get us a quantity of orders per order status.

3. Check the box next to **I understand that this API endpoint will change data** and then click **Run**.

4. Go to the **Response** tab (*Figure 10.3*) to make sure there are no errors, and make a note of your query ID ({"id": "37") – we will need it later. Please note: the ID number is unique to you.

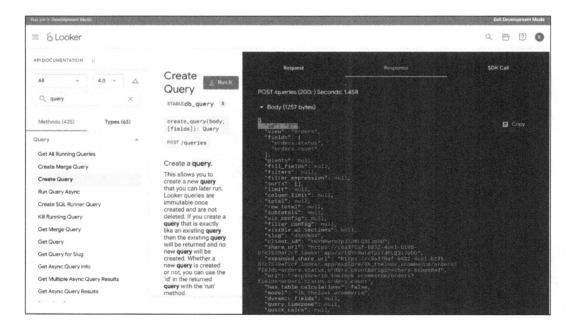

Figure 10.3 – Run It – Response

5. In the **Methods** list, search for the Run Query method. In the **Request** tab of the Run Query method, enter query_id, which is 37 in our case (you might have a different number). Then, enter csv for result_format and limit 10. (If you are curious, check the result formats available here: https://developers.looker.com/api/explorer/4.0/methods/Query/run_query?sdk=go.)

6. Scroll down and click **Run**.

7. Check the **Response** tab to see whether you have got your result with orders quantity per status.

8. Check the **SDK Call** tab that provides code snippets ready to copy and paste in multiple programming languages.

How it works...

APIs ensure smooth communication and efficient interactions between Looker and third-party applications. If a Looker developer wants to manage Looker from their Python notebook, they can easily do it through the APIs. With Looker APIs, you can basically control Looker from your code.

Looker APIs unlock a world of programmatic possibilities for data manipulation and analysis. You can automate routine reporting tasks, dynamically integrate Looker data with external applications, or craft data-driven workflows. Looker APIs empower developers and data analysts to transcend manual processes and unlock the true potential of their information ecosystems. With a code-based approach, you can explore and use data in ways that weren't possible before, leading to new ideas and breakthroughs.

There's more...

To practice using the Looker API from a Python notebook, you can start from here: https://colab.research.google.com/github/looker-open-source/sdk-codegen/blob/main/python/python-sdk-tutorial.ipynb

To save your own version, click on the **Copy to Drive** button and start working through the instructions. You can also try in this notebook the blocks of code we created with the API Explorer earlier in this chapter.

See also

- Looker API Reference: https://cloud.google.com/looker/docs/reference/looker-api/latest

- Get familiar with Looker SDKs: https://developers.looker.com/api/getting-started

- Using the API Explorer: https://cloud.google.com/looker/docs/api-explorer

- SDK Codegen – Looker open source repository: `https://github.com/looker-open-source/sdk-codegen`

- Colab Looker SDK Tutorial:`https://colab.sandbox.google.com/github/looker-open- source/sdk-codegen/blob/main/python/python-sdk-tutorial.ipynb`

- API Articles & Tutorials: `https://developers.looker.com/api/tutorials/`

Embedding Looker

Looker's embed solution allows you to seamlessly integrate Looker dashboards, visualizations, and Explores into external applications and websites, bringing the power of data analysis to your own digital spaces. This means you can share your data insights and analysis beyond the Looker platform, directly enriching user experiences in other tools and platforms. You can embed Looker through an iframe or by leveraging the Embed SDK.

The iframe embedding options are as follows: private embedding, signed embedding, or signed embedding with the Embed SDK.

Getting ready

Open one of the Looker dashboards we created previously – for example, the one called **Ecommerce Dashboard** (or create a new dashboard following the instructions from *Chapter 4*). Open the URL `https://sites.google.com/` to create a free website that we will need to embed Looker (when opening Google Sites, make sure you are connected with the same Google account you are using for Looker).

How to do it...

Let's first explore the private embedding:

1. Open your Looker dashboard and click on three dots in the top-right corner of the dashboard (*Figure 10.4*).

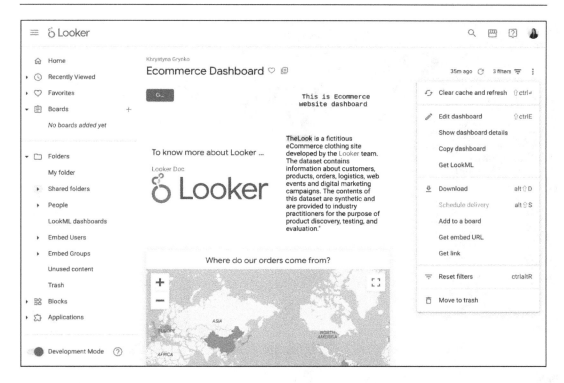

Figure 10.4 – Dashboard

2. In the drop-down list, find **Get Embed URL**, then click on **Copy Link**.

3. Open `https://sites.google.com/` and click on **+Start** to create a new site.

4. In the top-right corner of your empty Google site, click on **Embed**.

5. In the **Embed from the web** window, choose **By URL** and paste your copied Looker Embed URL (*Figure 10.5*).

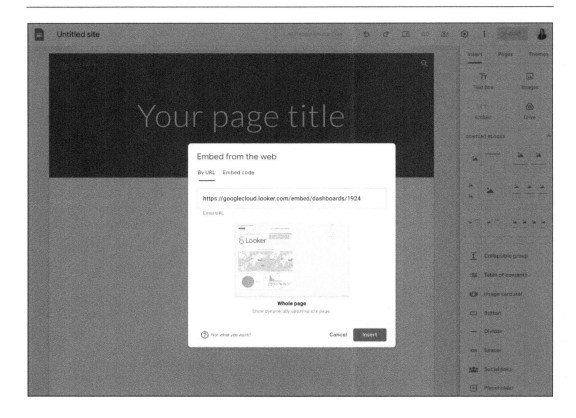

Figure 10.5 – Google Sites

6. Click **Insert**.

If you are not happy with how the dashboard is displayed, you can do the following:

1. Modify the dashboard in the Looker interface.

2. Embed the dashboard differently by choosing **Embed code** (and not **By URL**) and then adding iframe parameters. See the following, for example:

```
<iframe
    src="(add your Embed URL here)"
    width="600"
    height="3600"
    frameborder="0">
</iframe>
```

> **Reminder**
>
> To view embedded content, users must first log in to Looker in the same browser. Authentication is required through Looker built-in login system, Google OAuth, OpenID Connect, SAML, and LDAP. You can manage the unauthenticated user experience by choosing between error messages or a dedicated login screen (add the parameter `allow_login_screen=true` to your embed URL to display a login screen for users who are not yet logged in). You can control the session duration and inactivity timeouts for logged-in users through the 'Sessions' Admin panel.

How it works...

Looker embedding helps you to share dashboards, visualizations, or explorable data directly within your own workflows. You can simply generate an embed URL and integrate it into your web page or application using either a basic iframe approach or the more flexible Looker Embed SDK. Public (public access is available only for Looks) or private access options ensure control over who can view the embedded content. Once live, users interact with the embedded data as if they were within Looker itself, maintaining a consistent and intuitive experience. This powerful feature extends Looker's reach beyond its platform, empowering you to share data insights and drive informed decision-making directly within the context of your own applications.

There's more...

For greater flexibility and customization in your embedded analytics, explore our signed embedding options. Signed embedding lets you seamlessly integrate private Looks, visualizations, Explores, and dashboards directly into your application with users being authenticated through your own application (this differs from private embedding, which requires users to authenticate using a Looker login, Google OAuth, OpenID Connect, etc.).

Check the following website as an example of a website built with Looker using signed embedding (click the **Code** button in the bottom-right corner of the app to view how it was built): `https://atomfashion.io/`

To enable signed embedding you must use the Embed edition of Looker. More info on signed embedding can be found at `https://cloud.google.com/looker/docs/signed-embedding`.

There are even more advanced capabilities available with Looker embeddings:

- You can use JavaScript to make your page respond to what's happening in the embedded content, or even change it.
- You can track the embed usage.

- You can embed Looker content into systems such as Salesforce.

- Read more about the advanced embedding here: `https://developers.looker.com/embed/advanced-embedding`

See also

- Looker embed solution overview: `https://cloud.google.com/looker/docs/embed-overview` and `https://developers.looker.com/embed/getting-started`

- Security best practices for embedded analytics: `https://cloud.google.com/looker/docs/security-best-practices-embedded-analytics`

- Embedding Looker Content into Salesforce: `https://developers.looker.com/embed/advanced-embedding/embedding-salesforce`

Exploring the Looker extension framework

Looker extensions are like customizable apps built right into Looker, designed to enhance its functionality and deliver tailored experiences to users. They are like mini-apps that seamlessly integrate within Looker, expanding its capabilities and adapting it to specific needs. LookML Diagram and Data Dictionary, explored earlier in this book, are examples of Looker extensions.

The Looker extension framework is the structure and toolkit that empowers developers to create custom extensions within Looker. It allows third-party JavaScript to be hosted and run in Looker with context and privileged access to Looker APIs.

In this section, we'll explore the key concepts and tools within the framework, setting the stage for future application development.

Getting ready

This section will focus on the general steps applicable to the extension development. While specific instructions won't be provided here, following these generic steps will equip you with a solid understanding of the process. By the end of this section, you'll find useful links to detailed documentation on how to develop your Looker applications.

To develop a Looker extension, ensure you have the following:

- LookML developer permissions for the instance

- The extension framework feature enabled (**Admin->Platform->Extension Framework**)

- Familiarity with JavaScript

How to do it...

Here's a general outline of the steps involved in creating a Looker extension:

Start by creating a new starter extension from a template. It involves the following steps:

1. Configure Looker for extensions by creating a LookML project connected to Git with some model and project manifest files.

2. Install Yarn, an open source package manager, on your application server through a command-line tool

3. With the help of Yarn, install the **create-looker-extension** utility (it contains all the necessary elements for a basic Looker extension).

4. Start developing the extension in the Yarn development server by modifying the **src** directory. Your extension's source code lives in the **src** directory. To change how your extension works, edit the files within this directory. For example, in a React/JavaScript *Hello World* extension, you'd modify the `HelloWorld.js` file.

5. Copy the contents of your `manifest.lkml` file on the Yarn server to the `manifest.lkml` file in your LookML project, then go to **Validate LookML -> Commit Changes & Push -> Deploy to Production**.

6. The new extension will appear in your Looker instance's Applications panel (*Figure 10.6*). This official documentation page dives deep into creating an extension from a template: `https://cloud.google.com/looker/docs/extension-intro-to-building`

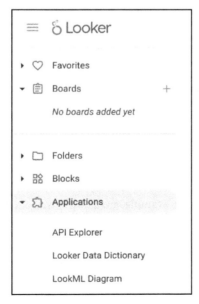

Figure 10.6 – Applications

7. To tailor the created starter extension to your specific needs, add code that unlocks the features and functionality you seek. This official documentation page provides some code examples with common functions you might want to use: `https://cloud.google.com/looker/docs/extension-framework-react-and-js-code-examples`

8. Make sure to provide all the necessary permissions to the extension users, such as the following permissions:

    I.   Develop the extension (in Looker: LookML developer permissions to the instance)

    II.   Install the extension (in Looker: develop, manage_models, and deploy permissions for the extension's model)

    III. Use the extension (in Looker: explore or develop permissions, Model Set access set to All)

This official documentation page dives deep into setting permissions for Looker extensions: `https://cloud.google.com/looker/docs/setting-permissions-for-extensions`

There's more...

To access a rich collection of customizable and advanced templates, simply visit the Looker extension framework examples repository. There, you'll find a variety of extensions that can be easily cloned and repurposed to serve as the perfect starting point for your project: `https://github.com/looker-open-source/extension-examples`

See also

*   Looker for Developers – Extensions: `https://developers.looker.com/extensions/overview`

Exploring components

React-based Looker components allow you to seamlessly blend Looker's design and functionality into your custom data applications and extensions. You can use Looker's pre-made React components for forms, buttons, charts, tables, and more. It's like a box of Looker building blocks.

You can use the components with both the Looker extension framework and Looker's Embed SDK.

Looker's visualization components, for example, are another way of embedding Looker content into the application.

Getting ready

This section will focus on the general steps applicable to the components' usage. While specific instructions won't be provided here, following these generic steps will equip you with a solid understanding of the process. By the end of this section, you'll find useful links to detailed documentation to work with Looker components.

The following are the key concepts involved in working with Looker components:

- Looker components are published to NPM, the package manager for JavaScript.
- NPM helps you to add Looker components to your frontend JavaScript or TypeScript app.
- NPM packages are available for UI, filter, and visualization components. These packages can be downloaded from the @looker/components NPM repository.
- You can use Yarn (mentioned in the previous section) to install Looker components as well.

How to do it...

Here's a general outline of the steps involved in using a Looker component:

1. Get the information about the Looker element you want to use in your app (for example, for an Explore, you might need the Explore ID that can be found in the URL)

2. Create a JS application (note that Looker components can be used directly within Looker extensions. This provides an easy way to leverage Looker's UI elements without needing to build a separate JavaScript application https://cloud.google.com/looker/docs/extension-intro-to-building). In this application, do the following:

    I.   Install all the necessary Looker component packages.

    II. Configure the environment variables.

    III. Initialize the SDKs.

    IV. Embed Looker components into the app.

    V.   Build the backend helper service that will receive the call from the frontend.

3. In Admin's Platform panel in Embed, you might need to add your application URL to **Embedded Domain Allowlist**.

4. Start the server and the React app.

See also

- Looker components overview: `https://cloud.google.com/looker/docs/components-overview`

- Visualization components: `https://developers.looker.com/components/visualization-components/`

- Looker UI components: `https://looker-open-source.github.io/components/latest/?path=/docs/home--docs`

- Looker Visualization Components on GitHub: `https://github.com/looker-open-source/components/tree/main/packages/visualizations`

Exploring the Looker Marketplace

Remember the valuable apps, visualizations, and data models (blocks) you found in the Looker Marketplace previously in this book? You can actually contribute to these resources yourself. For example, you can use the power of the extension framework, covered earlier, to build custom applications and share them with the Looker community through the Marketplace. You can also develop your own blocks and custom visualizations, adding them to the Marketplace to share with others.

Getting ready

This section will focus on the general steps applicable to Marketplace development. While specific instructions won't be provided here, following these generic steps will equip you with a solid understanding of the process. By the end of this section, you'll find useful links to detailed documentation to develop for the Looker Marketplace.

How to do it...

A Looker block is a pre-built data model designed for common analytical patterns and data sources, providing a quicker starting point for data analysis in Looker. Developing a Looker block for the Marketplace involves the following steps:

1. Connect Looker to the data source you will be building your block for (don't forget to write the requirements to the data source schema to make your block work for other users).

2. Create the LookML project that will contain your block with the following files: `manifest`, `view`, `model`, `explore`, LookML dashboard, `marketplace.json`, `LICENSE`, and `README` files. When the user installs your block from the Marketplace, it will contain those files and the autogenerated files.

3. Make your block available to all users by hosting it in a publicly accessible Git repository.

4. Submit the block for review.

More about developing a Looker block can be found here: `https://cloud.google.com/looker/docs/marketplace-develop-custom-blocks`

Creating Looker Custom Visualizations

Developing a Looker custom visualization for a Marketplace involves the following steps:

1. Build your custom visualization in your JavaScript environment using the Looker Visualization API.

2. Create a LookML project with the following files: `LICENSE`, `README`, `.js`, `manifest.lkml`, and `marketplace.json`.

3. Push your project to a publicly accessible GitHub repository.

4. Test the functionality of your custom visualization.

5. Submit the visualization for review.

More about developing a Looker custom visualization can be found here: `https://cloud.google.com/looker/docs/marketplace-develop-visualization`

There's more...

Check this online interactive Looker custom visualization builder to help you build and debug your custom visualization: `https://looker-open-source.github.io/custom-viz-builder/`

See also

- Looker Marketplace overview: `https://cloud.google.com/looker/docs/marketplace-overview`

- Developing for the Looker Marketplace: `https://cloud.google.com/looker/docs/marketplace-develop`

- Looker for Developers – Marketplace: `https://developers.looker.com/marketplace/overview/`

Index

packtpub.com

Subscribe to our online digital library for full access to over 7,000 books and videos, as well as industry leading tools to help you plan your personal development and advance your career. For more information, please visit our website.

Why subscribe?

- Spend less time learning and more time coding with practical eBooks and Videos from over 4,000 industry professionals

- Improve your learning with Skill Plans built especially for you

- Get a free eBook or video every month

- Fully searchable for easy access to vital information

- Copy and paste, print, and bookmark content

Did you know that Packt offers eBook versions of every book published, with PDF and ePub files available? You can upgrade to the eBook version at packtpub.com and as a print book customer, you are entitled to a discount on the eBook copy. Get in touch with us at customercare@packtpub.com for more details.

At www.packtpub.com, you can also read a collection of free technical articles, sign up for a range of free newsletters, and receive exclusive discounts and offers on Packt books and eBooks.

Other Books You May Enjoy

If you enjoyed this book, you may be interested in these other books by Packt:

Database Design and Modeling with Google Cloud

Abirami Sukumaran

ISBN: 978-1-80461-145-6

- Understand different use cases and real-world applications of data in the cloud
- Work with document and indexed NoSQL databases
- Get to grips with modeling considerations for analytics, AI, and ML
- Use real-world examples to learn about ETL services
- Design structured, semi-structured, and unstructured data for your applications and analytics
- Improve observability, performance, security, scalability, latency SLAs, SLIs, and SLOs

Data Engineering with Google Cloud Platform

Adi Wijaya

ISBN: 978-1-80056-132-8

- Load data into BigQuery and materialize its output for downstream consumption
- Build data pipeline orchestration using Cloud Composer
- Develop Airflow jobs to orchestrate and automate a data warehouse
- Build a Hadoop data lake, create ephemeral clusters, and run jobs on the Dataproc cluster
- Leverage Pub/Sub for messaging and ingestion for event-driven systems
- Use Dataflow to perform ETL on streaming data
- Unlock the power of your data with Data Studio
- Calculate the GCP cost estimation for your end-to-end data solutions

Data Storytelling with Google Looker Studio

Sireesha Pulipati

ISBN: 978-1-80056-876-1

- Understand what storytelling with data means, and explore its various forms
- Discover the 3D approach to building dashboards – determine, design, and develop
- Test common data visualization pitfalls and learn how to mitigate them
- Get up and running with Looker Studio and leverage it to explore and visualize data
- Explore the advanced features of Looker Studio with examples
- Become well-versed in the step-by-step process of the 3D approach using practical examples
- Measure and monitor the usage patterns of your Looker Studio reports

Packt is searching for authors like you

If you're interested in becoming an author for Packt, please visit `authors.packtpub.com` and apply today. We have worked with thousands of developers and tech professionals, just like you, to help them share their insight with the global tech community. You can make a general application, apply for a specific hot topic that we are recruiting an author for, or submit your own idea.

Share Your Thoughts

Now you've finished *Business Intelligence with Looker Cookbook*, we'd love to hear your thoughts! Scan the QR code below to go straight to the Amazon review page for this book and share your feedback or leave a review on the site that you purchased it from.

`https://packt.link/r/1-800-56095-8`

Your review is important to us and the tech community and will help us make sure we're delivering excellent quality content.

Download a free PDF copy of this book

Thanks for purchasing this book!

Do you like to read on the go but are unable to carry your print books everywhere?

Is your e-book purchase not compatible with the device of your choice?

Don't worry!, Now with every Packt book, you get a DRM-free PDF version of that book at no cost.

Read anywhere, any place, on any device. Search, copy, and paste code from your favorite technical books directly into your application.

The perks don't stop there, you can get exclusive access to discounts, newsletters, and great free content in your inbox daily

Follow these simple steps to get the benefits:

1. Scan the QR code or visit the following link:

https://packt.link/free-ebook/9781800560956

2. Submit your proof of purchase.
3. That's it! We'll send your free PDF and other benefits to your email directly.